WHERE THE WORLD MEETS TO PRAY

Daniele Och
UK editor

INVITATIONAL
INTERDENOMINATIONAL
INTERNATIONAL

36 LANGUAGES
Multiple formats are available in some languages

BRF

15 The Chambers, Vineyard
Abingdon OX14 3FE
brf.org.uk

Bible Reading Fellowship (BRF) is a charity (233280)
and company limited by guarantee (301324),
registered in England and Wales

ISBN 978 1 80039 187 1

Originally published in the USA by The Upper Room® upperroom.org
US edition © 2022 The Upper Room, Nashville, TN (USA). All rights reserved.
This edition © Bible Reading Fellowship 2022
Cover image © pexels.com/@pixabay

Acknowledgements

Scripture quotations marked with the following abbreviations are taken from the version shown. Where no abbreviation is given, the quotation is taken from the same version as the headline reference.

NIV: The Holy Bible, New International Version (Anglicised edition) copyright © 1979, 1984, 2011 by Biblica. Used by permission of Hodder & Stoughton Publishers, an Hachette UK company. All rights reserved. 'NIV' is a registered trademark of Biblica. UK trademark number 1448790.

NRSV: The New Revised Standard Version of the Bible, Anglicised Edition, copyright © 1989, 1995 by the Division of Christian Education of the National Council of the Churches of Christ in the USA. Used by permission. All rights reserved.

CEB: copyright © 2011 by Common English Bible.

KJV: the Authorised Version of the Bible (The King James Bible), the rights in which are vested in the Crown, are reproduced by permission of the Crown's Patentee, Cambridge University Press.

A catalogue record for this book is available from the British Library

Printed by Gutenberg Press, Tarxien, Malta

How to use *The Upper Room*

The Upper Room is ideal in helping us spend a quiet time with God each day. Each daily entry is based on a passage of scripture and is followed by a meditation and prayer. Each person who contributes a meditation to the magazine seeks to relate their experience of God in a way that will help those who use *The Upper Room* every day.

Here are some guidelines to help you make best use of *The Upper Room*:

1 Read the passage of scripture. It is a good idea to read it more than once, in order to have a fuller understanding of what it is about and what you can learn from it.
2 Read the meditation. How does it relate to your own experience? Can you identify with what the writer has outlined from their own experience or understanding?
3 Pray the written prayer. Think about how you can use it to relate to people you know or situations that need your prayers today.
4 Think about the contributor who has written the meditation. Some users of *The Upper Room* include this person in their prayers for the day.
5 Meditate on the 'Thought for the day' and the 'Prayer focus', perhaps using them again as the focus for prayer or direction for action.

Why is it important to have a daily quiet time? Many people will agree that it is the best way of keeping in touch every day with the God who sustains us and who sends us out to do his will and show his love to the people we encounter each day. Meeting with God in this way reassures us of his presence with us, helps us to discern his will for us and makes us part of his worldwide family of Christian people through our prayers.

I hope that you will be encouraged as you use the magazine regularly as part of your daily devotions, and that God will richly bless you as you read his word and seek to learn more about him.

Daniele Och
UK editor

Helping to pay it forward

Caring for our gifts

When [the wise men] saw that the star had stopped, they were overwhelmed with joy. On entering the house, they saw the child with Mary his mother; and they knelt down and paid him homage. Then, opening their treasure-chests, they offered him gifts of gold, frankincense, and myrrh.
Matthew 2:10–11 (NRSV)

The climactic scene of the magi story is when the travellers kneel before Jesus in worship and present their gifts. Many sermons have been preached and many texts have been written on the identity of the magi and the possible meanings of the gifts. But I want to invite us to focus on the simple fact that the gifts made it to the little house in Bethlehem whole and intact. This feat wasn't an accident. It surely took planning and care to protect the valuable gifts throughout the long journey.

During the season of Epiphany, we celebrate not only the gifts of the magi but also the gifts of the Holy Spirit among the people of God. These are gifts for the building up of the body of Christ and for the gospel work of restoration and reconciliation in our world. Every follower of Christ has been endowed with gifts and abilities that we are called to nurture, protect and use as we present ourselves as living sacrifices to God (see Romans 12:1). During this season may God 'fully satisfy every need of yours according to [God's] riches in glory in Christ Jesus' (Philippians 4:19).

Revd Kimberly Orr
World editor and publisher

Ilokano
edition

Indonesian
edition

Philippines-English
edition

Writers featured in this issue of *The Upper Room*

- Linda Chandra (Indonesia) • Ayub Simanjuntak (Indonesia)
- Waspati Ken Wardani (Indonesia) • Renaldo Yosua (Indonesia)
- Dave Zyronn A. Escalona (The Philippines)
- Kong Peng Sun (Singapore) • Agnes Wee (Singapore)

Gifts to the international editions of
The Upper Room help the world meet to pray.
upperroom.org/gift

The editor writes...

Also in front of the throne there was what looked like a sea of glass, clear as crystal.
Revelation 4:6 (NIV)

I was born and raised in the southern hemisphere, so for most of my life Christmastide and New Year was not 'the bleak midwinter' but the height of summer. My summer holidays usually involved camping near the beach, and I would spend the days enjoying the sun, sand and surf. The joy, however, was always tempered with a good dose of awe and fear, for the sea – as I often heard on the news and sometimes experienced myself – is a dangerous place.

The sea as a place of danger is also the impression we get as we read the Bible. The writers of both testaments (in common with many other writers, ancient and modern) almost always associate the sea with chaos, threat and destruction. We see this especially in the account of creation in Genesis 1, in the stories of Noah, Moses and Jonah, and in the gospels and Acts. This is to be expected, of course, given that the sea by its nature (as we see on the front cover of this issue) is restless, unpredictable and turbulent. It is little wonder that by the end of the Bible, we read that in the new heaven and new earth 'there was no longer any sea' (Revelation 21:1).

Earlier in his apocalyptic vision, however, John does see that in front of the throne of heaven there is a sea – or at least what looks like a sea. It is a 'sea of glass, clear as crystal' (Revelation 4:6). Unlike the waters shown in our cover photo, this sea is smooth and still as glass; unlike the dark depths of the ocean where the light of the sun doesn't reach, this sea is clear and transparent. It is a picture of the absolute sovereignty of God.

And this, too, the Bible writers universally attest to – whether it's in the story of Noah and the ark, Jonah fleeing across the sea, Jesus crossing Lake Galilee or Paul's journey to Rome, the dangerous power of the sea is always contained within God's sovereign reign – and we therefore need not fear.

Appropriately for the beginning of a new year, this issue begins with a meditation entitled 'Change'. As I write this in the (northern) summer time, I do not know what changes you and I and the world at large will have experienced by the time you read this. But one thing is certain – our God reigns, and he promises that 'the earth will be filled with the knowledge of the Lord, as the waters cover the sea' (Isaiah 11:9).

Daniele Och
UK editor

Change

Read Ecclesiastes 3:1–11
There is a time for everything.
Ecclesiastes 3:1 (NIV)

You know what I like about the autumn? It is the season of change. The hot season starts cooling, and we can feel a change in ourselves as well. Sometimes the change is physical or mental, and sometimes we change spiritually.

This past week the weather really couldn't make up its mind. On a cool Friday afternoon, I was on the bus home from school and I found myself looking out the window. I was thinking about how much the trees and nature had changed and how beautiful the changes were. And then I thought about how much I had changed, how my family and my friends had changed and how beautiful those changes are too. And God is working in these transitions to make our lives even more beautiful.

Change happens around us, within us and sometimes right in front of us. Sometimes things change in strange ways, but in the end, the change reveals God's work in the world.

Prayer: *God, thank you for all that you have done for us and in us. We pray that you keep changing the world, the future and our lives. Amen*

Thought for the day: I can choose to embrace change as a gift from God.

Asher Broome (Georgia, USA)

Our refuge

Read Psalm 34:1–7

This poor man called, and the Lord heard him; he saved him out of all his troubles.
Psalm 34:6 (NIV)

I was going through a difficult time in my life which often made me feel hopeless and afraid. I was ashamed of my feelings, because I thought that as a Christian I should have a better response to my problems. Amid my hopelessness and fear, I was reminded of the words of David and the other authors of the psalms. Their words are honest and heartfelt, and meditating on the Psalms has helped me to be more honest with God about my feelings.

God desires a deeper relationship with us, and through our relationship with God we are comforted and encouraged to keep going. God is our refuge.

Though our problems may be overwhelming and beyond our control, we can rest assured that the God of Jacob is with us. As we read in Psalm 46, we need only to be still and acknowledge God's power and presence.

Prayer: *Lord God, you know the problems we are going through. Help us to share our feelings honestly with you, our safe place. Amen*

Thought for the day: I can find comfort in God when I honestly share my feelings.

Deborah Priyali (Telangana, India)

Restoration

Read Joel 2:21–27

'I will repay you for the years the locusts have eaten… you will praise the name of the Lord your God, who has worked wonders for you.'
Joel 2:25–26 (NIV)

Have you ever restored a vehicle? In our family, vehicle restoration has become a bit of a passion. There is something rather glorious about an old, rusty tractor, car or trailer being given new life. But it takes time, patience and a lot of setbacks. Sometimes, whole parts of a vehicle may need to be taken off or stripped down before it can be put back together in working order.

In today's rather dramatic passage, Joel speaks of hope after devastation, and of the ultimate restoration of God's relationship with his people. Sadly, our world experiences plenty of situations that are as dramatic as those described in Joel: war, famine, homelessness, violence, poverty, disease – all of these are spread across the world. We also find in our own lives that we go through times of desolation, trauma or grief that threaten to envelop us.

While we hold these things in our hearts, within us also beats the hope that Joel speaks of here: God does not abandon us in despair. He works wonders in our lives! He will renew and restore the things that are lost and broken, whether in this world or ultimately in his heavenly kingdom.

Perhaps we are a little like an abandoned vehicle, but God has the patience and creativity to restore us in all our glory.

Prayer: *Lord, thank you for your hope, and that you work wonders in our lives. Amen*

Thought for the day: In Christ, I am a new creation (see 2 Corinthians 5:17).

Amy Turner (England, United Kingdom)

Setting the tone

Read James 2:14–26

My brothers and sisters, what good is it if people say they have faith but do nothing to show it? Claiming to have faith can't save anyone, can it?
James 2:14 (CEB)

During my teen years, I was looking for meaning in life. I had recently moved from a small town to a big city, and I didn't know many people. I started attending a church, where I met a woman almost 50 years my senior. She invited me to dinner and showed me how to become a believer in Jesus Christ. For the next three years, she and her husband made me a part of their family. I enjoyed many meals and activities with them, cared for their house when they went on holiday and took trips with them. During that time I was also part of a weekly Bible study group for young adults.

Those first three years of my Christian life set the tone for how I would live out my Christian faith. Eventually I had to leave that church to attend school in another town. I asked my dear friend, 'How can I ever thank you for all you have done for me?' She answered, 'Do it for someone else.' And that's what I have sought to do.

Prayer: *Dear Lord, help us not only to tell others about our faith but also to show them what it looks like. Amen*

Thought for the day: How can I show someone I meet today what a genuine Christian life looks like?

Irene Robinson (Gauteng, South Africa)

Let your light shine

Read Exodus 34:28–32

When Moses came down from Mount Sinai with the two tablets of the covenant law in his hands, he was not aware that his face was radiant because he had spoken with the Lord.
Exodus 34:29 (NIV)

Life with young children is a blessing, but it can also be challenging. My wife and I have worked diligently over the years to manage our busy schedule while making sure to incorporate plenty of time with our children in the process.

One of our family activities is grocery shopping. Every other Saturday we drive to a bustling market where the aisles seem more like highway traffic jams. With the girls in the cart, we go up and down the aisles, dodging other shoppers while my wife grabs our items and marks them off the list.

A few weeks ago as we were shopping, a man stopped me to compliment my beautiful family. He noticed our playful nature as we sped up and down the busy aisles of the market. His words sank directly into my heart, and I knew God was to thank for them.

When we spend time with God regularly, we will radiate God's goodness, just as Moses did. The joy this man noticed in our family was a result of our time spent with God. Despite our busyness, we can allow God to fill our lives with divine radiance. Just as Moses discovered, we can find great joy in spending time with the Lord.

Prayer: *Dear Lord, help us to radiate your love to others, wherever we are and wherever we go. Amen*

Thought for the day: I will carry God's light with me everywhere I go.

Zach Schaar (Ohio, USA)

Can you hear it?

Read 1 Kings 19:11–18

After the earthquake came a fire, but the Lord was not in the fire. And after the fire came a gentle whisper. When Elijah heard it, he pulled his cloak over his face and went out and stood at the mouth of the cave.
1 Kings 19:12–13 (NIV)

I enjoy eating yoghurt in the morning. My cat, Cali, also loves yoghurt, but she is often curled in a sunspot in another part of the house when I am ready to eat. No matter where she is, she comes running whenever she hears the small sound of my peeling back the cover of the yoghurt.

Over the years I have wondered how to hear God's voice and call in my life. I tune into God's loving presence by reading the Bible and *The Upper Room*, journalling, spending time in community with my church family, talking and sharing with friends, and praying. And Cali's response to my small sound each morning makes me realise that when I pay attention, I can 'hear' God's voice.

I hear God in a Bible verse or a devotion that resonates or a journal entry that reveals a hidden truth. God's voice is in a phrase from a sermon that stays in my heart and in conversations that suddenly create a deeper spiritual connection to God. When I am in prayer or even just silent and listening, I hear the still small voice of God. And if I respond to God's voice, I know good things are waiting for me.

Prayer: *Dear God, your voice is everywhere and in everything. Help us to listen carefully and respond faithfully. Amen*

Thought for the day: What helps me to listen for God's voice?

Patricia Kinner Kelly (Florida, USA)

In community

Read 1 Corinthians 12:12–26

Just as the body is one and has many members, and all the members of the body, though many, are one body, so it is with Christ.
1 Corinthians 12:12 (NRSV)

When I was invited by my husband to go shopping for building materials at a hardware store, I saw the many different types of materials used to make buildings. I realised how many materials are required to build a house, including sand, cement, bricks, nails, tile and wall paint, to name just a few.

Indeed, the materials we bought do not look like they will form a building. But in the hands of skilled builders, the raw materials will come together to form a beautiful house.

Likewise, it seems that as Christians our purpose may be difficult to determine alone. But if we join with other Christians in community, our purpose becomes clearer. Christians need one another. Some lead worship, some play music, some share God's word and so on. This wonderful unity strengthens us. It is beautiful when Christians build each other up and work together to serve God.

Prayer: *Dear God, thank you for the fellowship of other Christians. Help us to build each other up and find unity in our faith communities. Amen*

Thought for the day: I am best able to serve God when I spend time in faithful community.

Ruth Sri Ningsih (East Java, Indonesia)

Setbacks

Read Romans 5:1–5

Suffering produces endurance, and endurance produces character...
because God's love has been poured into our hearts through the Holy
Spirit that has been given to us.
Romans 5:3–5 (NRSV)

As I stood near the top of a mountain near Lake Tahoe, California, my
hands were shaking. My fingers felt numb, and my teeth began to chat-
ter. At mile 22, I had submerged underwater as part of a 30-mile obstacle
course race, and the wind blowing into my face caused my wet hair
to freeze.

My mind was spinning. *I can't do this. I need to quit.* Others were feeling the same effects, but they kept pushing forward. Up ahead I could
see an emergency vehicle. Though continuing might mean a fulfilling
accomplishment, I had to quit. The comfort of the medical tent felt amazing, but that feeling was quickly replaced with shame and frustration.

Jesus knows our challenges and can help us use our setbacks to
reshape our life's trajectory. He allows our most disappointing times
to serve as catalysts for greatness. I was faced with a critical decision
on that mountain: would this be my last race, or would I learn from my
failure to properly prepare my body and mind for the next? Choosing the
latter allowed me the opportunity for redemption. Crossing the finish
line the following year was an incredible feeling and taught me a great
lesson – all to God's glory!

Prayer: *Dear God, help us to embrace the challenges that come our*
way and to see them as opportunities to place our trust in you. Amen

Thought for the day: Disappointments are opportunities to trust
God.

Stuart Stein (South Dakota, USA)

Small steps of faith

Read Joshua 1:3–9

Commit your way to the Lord! Trust him!
Psalm 37:5 (CEB)

I love to plan for what is going to happen in the coming weeks or months.
I also tend to get stuck in a rut doing the same ministry with people
I already know. But recently I felt God leading me to try something new.

God wanted me to take a small step of faith. Even though I knew
I would be out of my comfort zone, I trusted that God would give me the
strength and guidance to complete whatever God asked me to do. That
day my step of faith was to visit someone I didn't know very well. I was
really nervous, but I trusted God and went. I found the older woman was
personable but very lonely. We had a wonderful chat. I was thankful that
I went to visit her. I felt blessed by our conversation, and I hope she felt
the same. That visit was the first step of many more small steps of faith.

When we allow God to lead us in new directions, God will show us
small steps of faith that can make a world of difference.

Prayer: *Almighty Father, lead us in new steps of faith, and give us
courage as we step out of our comfort zones to serve you. We pray as
your Son taught us, 'Father, hallowed be your name, your kingdom
come. Give us each day our daily bread. Forgive us our sins, for
we also forgive everyone who sins against us. And lead us not into
temptation' (Luke 11:2–4, NIV). Amen*

Thought for the day: With small steps of faith, I can make a world
of difference.

Kathleen R. Brewer (New Brunswick, Canada)

Willing to learn

Read Leviticus 19:1–15

Do not curse the deaf or put a stumbling block in front of the blind.
Leviticus 19:14 (NIV)

Until several people who are visually impaired joined our church, I had never given Leviticus 19:14 much thought. But when these people joined our fellowship, they suggested ways to make our church more accessible. They helped us realise that while we had never intentionally put an object in a blind person's path, some of our usual ways could cause difficulties for our members who are visually impaired.

Thankfully, our friends have patiently coached us as we have learned how to assist them while still respecting their independence. One member named Thom told me, 'Be my eyes, not my brain.' With this in mind, I learned to describe choices as we move through the buffet line instead of making decisions for him. I now include a description on my social media posts instead of only a picture. And I ask others how they would like to help during church events instead of assuming they can't participate.

Every member is significant in the body of Christ. God provides guidance to help us learn from one another as we worship and serve God together.

Prayer: *Dear Lord, help us to learn from one another as we join together to serve and worship you. Amen*

Thought for the day: How am I a stumbling block in the body of Christ?

Lori Hatcher (South Carolina, USA)

Unexpected ways

Read 1 Corinthians 10:31–33

I am not seeking my own good but the good of many, so that they may be saved.

1 Corinthians 10:33 (NIV)

I was feeling lost and out of place. I was sure that I had chosen the wrong place to go to university and spent hours trying to convince my mum that I needed to transfer or come home for a year. I prayed daily for a sign to tell me to leave.

I decided, however, to stay one more semester, and I moved in with a new roommate. During the first week of classes, my roommate began opening up to me. She told me that she had been struggling with her faith and that she had noticed my strong faith in Christ. She believed God had placed me in her life so that she would seek her own relationship with Christ.

When we pray, we often expect God to grant our requests in just the way we ask. But in that moment I realised that while I was praying and asking God to give me a new start, to give me what I thought I needed, God was doing just that but in a different way than I had imagined. I had been so worried about finding contentment in my surroundings I had forgotten that joy can only be found in Christ. As a Christian, no matter where I am, my purpose is to lead others to Jesus.

Prayer: *Dear God, set our hearts on you so that everything we do may be in your name and for your glory. Amen*

Thought for the day: God's answers to my prayers may be different than I expect.

Savannah Ashley Smith (North Carolina, USA)

Trusting God

Read Luke 1:26–45

'Nothing will be impossible with God.'
Luke 1:37 (NRSV)

A brilliant shock of lightning flashed across the pitch-dark sky. A deafening thunderclap followed. I trembled, feeling exposed and vulnerable as the light flashed through the cracks of the grass-thatched mud house where we slept. I wedged myself into a corner to evade the raindrops of the heavy downpour. I momentarily forgot about my hunger, even though I had eaten only porridge for dinner. Sleeping with an empty stomach was common in our family. I was overwhelmed by a feeling of hopelessness.

'Musee,' my prayerful grandmother mumbled, 'don't worry about our current state; trust God who created you, for nothing is impossible with God. You will own a decent shelter and eat to your fill.' Our devout grandmother Kiima advised us to work hard and to trust in God. She said God would deliver us. 'But how? When?' I asked. Nonetheless, I believed her; I trusted God, and I worked hard.

God has been faithful. Despite hardships, I passed my school examinations. I enrolled in a renowned university and graduated with a first-class honours degree. Our family now lives decently, and I am writing a thesis for my master's degree in communication studies. What a testament to God's power! Even when life seems hopeless, we can have faith that nothing is impossible with God.

Prayer: *O God, help us to believe in your saving power. Amen*

Thought for the day: Even when life seems hopeless, I will trust God's power.

Festus Muinde (Nairobi, Kenya)

Eternal life

Read John 11:17–27

Jesus said to her, 'I am the resurrection and the life. The one who believes in me will live, even though they die; and whoever lives by believing in me will never die.'
John 11:25–26 (NIV)

My husband was discouraged and depressed. After treating him for breathing problems for several months, the doctors still could not make a diagnosis and weren't sure what the future held for him.

As a pastor, my husband had dedicated his life to serving others and walking with them through their dark valleys. Now he seemed lost and confused. I struggled to find ways to comfort him. But even reminiscing about family camping adventures we enjoyed over the years brought only temporary relief.

One day not long before he died, I walked into his hospital room and felt a peace not of this world. With a faint smile on his face, my husband turned to me and asked, 'Are you ready for the next great adventure?' He had accepted the reality of eternal life promised by Jesus when he said, 'I am the resurrection and the life. The one who believes in me will live, even though they die; and whoever lives by believing in me will never die.'

I now know in my heart what comfort that promise can give to those who struggle with the reality of their own approaching death, as well as to those left behind. The death of our earthly bodies is not the end. When we accept Jesus as our Saviour, a whole new great adventure awaits.

Prayer: *Dear Lord, thank you for your promise that we will remain with you even after our earthly life is over. Amen*

Thought for the day: Jesus' resurrection offers me the greatest sense of peace.

Nancy J. Clark (Michigan, USA)

How long?

Read Psalm 13

I trust in your unfailing love.
Psalm 13:5 (NIV)

Last autumn I planted four amaryllis bulbs. Three began to grow almost immediately, developing strong stems and sturdy buds, and I was able to give them to friends as Christmas gifts. The fourth bulb, however, sat in its pot and did nothing. Weeks went by with no sign of growth. I anxiously checked the soil and prodded the bulb. Still nothing. *Should I throw it away?* I wondered. I decided to wait. Then one day in mid-January, after all the other amaryllis flowers had bloomed and withered, a green tip appeared on the fourth bulb. After that day, the new shoot seemed to leap upward in its eagerness to grow.

We can't always see what God is doing. Sometimes we don't know whether God is doing anything at all, and that can be difficult. Through the centuries, people of faith have cried out in times of darkness, 'How long must we wait for help? Where is God? Has God heard my prayers? Does God care?'

The late-blooming amaryllis gives me hope. God *does* care. God *is* listening. Although we may not see it, life may be stirring deep down in hidden places. We can fret about our circumstances, or we can cry out to God, whose love is unfailing. Then we wait to see that first glimpse of green.

Prayer: *Father God, help us to remember that you are always with us, even in our waiting. Amen*

Thought for the day: Even when I can't see it, God is at work.

April McIntyre (England, United Kingdom)

Laying down my life

Read Ephesians 5:1–2

'Greater love has no one than this: to lay down one's life for one's friends.'
John 15:13 (NIV)

Since 2012, I have regularly donated blood. I started donating blood as a way to get over my fear of needles, but since then God has helped me to see my blood donations as a way to practise laying down my life for others.

John 15:13 says, 'Greater love has no one than this: to lay down one's life for one's friends.' I may never need to die for someone, but God gives us opportunities to offer a part of our lives in loving service to others. Giving blood is my way of doing this. Spending an hour of my time in this way has given me the opportunity to trust God to work in the lives of those in need. Although I don't know the outcome of any of my blood donations, I have faith that God has provided a life-saving gift through my willingness to offer just an hour of my life for the benefit of another person.

God calls each of us to show our love for others by offering ourselves in service. What gifts or talents do we have that could make a difference in someone's life? In whatever way we choose to answer God's call, we walk in obedience and trust that God will work through our living sacrifice.

Prayer: *Dear God, help us to trust and obey when you call us to sacrificial service for someone in need. In Jesus' name. Amen*

Thought for the day: Today I will joyfully lay down my life in service to God.

Michael Kimmel (Texas, USA)

No dead ends

Read Matthew 7:7–12

'These are the words of him who is holy and true, who holds the key of David. What he opens no one can shut, and what he shuts no one can open.'
Revelation 3:7 (NIV)

As I walked one morning, I pondered a seemingly impossible situation that my young grandson was facing at school. Up ahead I saw a 'Dead End' street sign and concrete wall. As I got closer, I noticed a metal door built into the wall and could hear the sound of heavy traffic. Opening the door, I saw that it led to the sidewalk of a main thoroughfare. The street was a dead end for cars, but on foot I could reach anywhere in town. I knew then that God could make a way through even though there seemed to be no way. I was reassured that God had an answer to my grandson's situation.

We often encounter situations that appear to be dead ends. We may slow our pace or turn around, fearful of what will happen when we reach the end. But with God, there are no dead ends. When we have courage and keep walking, God will show us the way through our difficulty.

Prayer: *Dear God, give us the courage to keep walking until we see the door you have opened for us. Amen*

Thought for the day: With God as my guide, every dead end leads to possibility.

Karen Dorsey (Oregon, USA)

Immanuel

Read Luke 24:13–35

When I look up at your skies, at what your fingers made – the moon and the stars… what are human beings that you pay attention to them?
Psalm 8:3–4 (CEB)

One night as I was brushing my hair before going to bed, I saw a reflection of the full moon in the mirror. Remembering Psalm 8, I felt a sense of well-being and peace. I went to the window to admire the moon but saw only the tree in my garden, its branches and leaves blocking the moonlight. I turned toward the mirror and the radiant reflection was still there. Looking out the window again, I searched intently to pinpoint the exact opening or space where the moonlight was coming through. Only darkness filled the garden. I could not see the moon even though I was sure I was looking in the right direction.

I thought about the story found in the gospel of Luke about the two disciples and their encounter on the Emmaus road. Wrapped up in their grief, they did not recognise the stranger who joined them. Just as I could not see the moon directly but saw its reflection, sometimes I forget that God is always there. Even when our circumstances cloud our vision, God will be there to walk beside us.

Prayer: *Living God, open our eyes and grant us the wisdom to discern your presence. Thank you for never leaving us alone. Amen*

Thought for the day: God may not be visible, but God is always with me.

Aris A. Román Silva (Puerto Rico)

A special place

Read Psalm 145:9–20

The peace of God, which passeth all understanding, shall keep your hearts and minds through Christ Jesus.
Philippians 4:7 (KJV)

Needing to find a quiet place to clear my head and find direction and peace, I had driven to one of my favourite spots. On a warm, breezy morning in southern New Jersey, I sat on a wooden bridge in the middle of the marshland, seeking an answer from God for a tough decision I had to make – a decision that could significantly affect the rest of my life. I prayed aloud, 'Lord, I need peace; please speak to me.' Though I have never heard an audible voice from God, there have been times that I have had a distinct impression or have had some evidence that I have interpreted as that 'still small voice of God' (see 1 Kings 19:12).

Shortly thereafter, a seagull landed in the creek which flowed under the bridge. It just sat there, peacefully looking at me as it floated in the water. Again I asked the Lord to speak. Looking around, I said, 'Oh, I see now. You *are* speaking. I'm just not listening!' All about me *was* peace. In the solitude, I sensed the Lord's voice and felt the beginning of peace in my mind and heart.

It's good to have a special place where we feel closest to the Lord. It is also always a good idea to pause and allow time for God to speak to us.

Prayer: *Dear Lord, we know that you are always here for us. Help us make time not only to talk with you but to listen for your still small voice of comfort. Amen*

Thought for the day: God is always willing to talk with me. Am I willing to listen?

Sam Siligato (New Jersey, USA)

Striving for humility

Read Matthew 23:1–12

'All who exalt themselves will be humbled, and all who humble themselves will be exalted.'
Matthew 23:12 (NRSV)

Last week, my friend and I had a heated disagreement. At first I didn't feel like I had anything to apologise for, but I was willing to let it go if my friend apologised. However, as I prayed about the situation, I realised that God was calling *me* to humble *myself* and tell my friend that I was sorry. But before I could call her, my friend called and apologised first. Unsettled feelings faded away, and our friendship was restored.

In Matthew 23, Jesus criticised the teachers of the law and the Pharisees for acting for show. Jesus calls his followers to be humble.

It can be hard to know what humility looks like in different contexts. Humility is being willing to apologise; it is quietly doing good deeds without expectation of compensation; it is listening to others with an open heart and mind, knowing there is always more to learn. Let us not exalt ourselves and try to appear better than others. May we instead strive for humility. Only then can we truly love others, and act as the hands and feet of Jesus in the world.

Prayer: *Lord Jesus, help us to humble ourselves so that we may better serve you. Amen*

Thought for the day: How is God calling me to demonstrate humility today?

Becca Wierwille (Pennsylvania, USA)

How to pray

Read Luke 18:15–17
Train children in the way they should go; when they grow old, they won't depart from it.
Proverbs 22:6 (CEB)

The six-year-old daughter of a church member once asked me three questions: Who taught you how to pray? Who teaches pastors how to pray? Can you teach me how to pray? I decided to teach her the two prayers my parents taught me when I was a child.

My parents thought it was important that my siblings and I learn two prayers that would become models for us to use even in our adult years – a prayer of gratitude before meals and the Lord's Prayer. I memorised these prayers as a child without fully understanding them. But as I grew older, the Lord's Prayer became a lifeline for me.

When the disciples asked Jesus to teach them how to pray, he taught them a model prayer that also provided them with guidance for how to live. And although Jesus taught the disciples the Lord's Prayer 2,000 years ago, it is still part of faithful practice in homes and churches around the world today. I have passed these model prayers on to my children and grandchildren, and I'm sure they will pass them to the next generations.

Prayer: *Loving God, thank you for children. Help us to nurture them with your word so that they may feel your presence in their life. Amen*

Thought for the day: Today I will try to live by the words of the Lord's Prayer.

Navamani Peter (Karnataka, India)

Finding the light

Read Psalm 18:25–36

Though I have fallen, I will rise. Though I sit in darkness, the Lord will be my light.
Micah 7:8 (NIV)

Several months after my college graduation, a few lumps formed in my neck. I had been sick and assumed my illness had caused my lymph nodes to swell, which is fairly common. But one day I woke up with a 102-degree fever, and my dad took me to the hospital. After days of waiting and praying, I received a cancer diagnosis at age 24. My faith was shaken, and I felt shrouded in darkness.

Even though my heart wasn't in it, I went to church each Sunday, knelt at the altar and cried out to God. The more I listened to sermons, Bible studies and participated in prayer groups, the more I saw God in everything and found meaning in God's words.

It is easy to trust God when everything is going well. But when something terrible happens, it is easier to turn our backs on God. Often when we experience grief and pain, we get lost in the struggle and cannot see God's guiding light. We may even fall away from our walk with God. But sometimes it is in those dark times that we can more clearly see the light of God shining through.

Prayer: *Dear God, give us the strength to see your guiding light through our darkest moments. Amen*

Thought for the day: Faithful practice helps me find the light of God.

Jenn Bailey (West Virginia, USA)

Two types of people

Read Mark 2:1–5

They couldn't carry him through the crowd, so they tore off part of the roof above where Jesus was. When they had made an opening, they lowered the mat on which the paralyzed man was lying.
Mark 2:4 (CEB)

Early in Jesus' ministry, he was preaching at a home. A large crowd gathered to hear him, many of whom had been healed of sickness by Jesus in the weeks before. Now they and many others returned to hear Jesus preach. It was so crowded that a group of people who brought a friend to be healed could not get anywhere near Jesus. So they climbed up to the roof of the house, cut a hole in it and lowered their friend down to Jesus.

As I considered the story, it seemed to me that there were two types of people in the story: those who wouldn't get out of the way so a man who needed Jesus could get to him, and those who would do anything to get their friend to Jesus. *Which one am I?* I wondered. I thought of the times I noticed people that need Jesus – at work, on the street, friends, family. God doesn't always ask us to cut a hole in the roof. Maybe we are called to offer a kind word, a meal, a listening ear or sometimes just to get out of the way. Now when I come upon a need, I ask Jesus to open my eyes and my heart so that I am helping and not standing in the way.

Prayer: *Dear God, open our eyes to those in need around us so that we can offer help in your name. Amen*

Thought for the day: With God's help, I will not hesitate to help those in need.

Jim Weems (Mississippi, USA)

Source of strength

Read 1 John 5:1–5

Whatsoever is born of God overcometh the world: and this is the victory that overcometh the world, even our faith.
1 John 5:4 (KJV)

A friend and I were having a chat a couple of days ago, and she asked, 'Is it wrong for a Christian to question God when things are hard and not making sense?' We all face tough times and ask, 'Why?'

I have certainly had moments when I have questioned God, not because I don't believe but because the situation just seems unbearable. I do not believe it's wrong to question God. The first disciples did, and so did many others throughout the Christian scriptures.

The past few years have been challenging for us all. We have been tested, frustrated and angry at our circumstances. But our reading from 1 John tells us who we are in Christ Jesus; we are 'overcomers'. And this truth will never change, even when things are bad. Because we are born of God, our source of strength lies in God. Knowing this doesn't always solve our immediate struggles, but it puts our minds at peace and enables us to continue to receive guidance from the Spirit of God. So 'in every thing give thanks: for this is the will of God in Christ Jesus concerning you' (1 Thessalonians 5:18).

Prayer: *Help us, O God, when we are at the crossroads of doubt and faith. May your word always shine as a beacon of light to us in our times of uncertainty. In Jesus' name. Amen*

Thought for the day: We are born of God, and therefore we can overcome.

Oluwaseun Ajia (Lagos, Nigeria)

Continuing education

Read Deuteronomy 17:14–20

[God] guides the humble in what is right and teaches them his way.
Psalm 25:9 (NIV)

I was a health-care clinician for 40 years. To maintain my credentials and remain in good standing, I had to provide my clinical board with annual proficiencies and continuing-education units. This was achieved by attending meetings, reading current articles, teaching or writing articles.

All of this ensures that practitioners are aware of the ever-changing field of medicine. We should never stop learning, growing and giving back to the profession.

I have discovered our faith walk is similar. We cannot rest on our laurels or think we are finished with learning and training. The words of the Bible do not change, but I have found that with each reading, the meaning applies in new ways to my ever-changing life. Growing our faith can happen in many ways – attending church and getting more involved, reading the Bible and devotionals, joining small groups, serving others. All of these are vital to the Christian walk. It is exciting to know that as we practise our faith, we continually deepen our relationship with God.

Prayer: *Sovereign God, thank you for your loving instructions in the Bible. Help us to learn from your word each time we read. In Jesus' name. Amen*

Thought for the day: There is always something new to learn in the life of faith.

Victor Carcioppolo (Ohio, USA)

Connections

Read 2 Corinthians 5:1–7
We live by faith, not by sight.
2 Corinthians 5:7 (NIV)

Making connections with students while teaching remotely is hard. I can't pat them on the back or easily whisper words of encouragement when they struggle. I can't offer high fives when they succeed. Instead I try to get to know my students when they share a project or when we eat lunch together online. Still it's hard not to feel disconnected.

One day after a reading lesson on character traits, I presented a slide with a picture of my face and asked my students to list some of my traits. Waiting anxiously, I wondered, *Will they be kind or brutally honest?* A quiet third-grade boy melted my heart by writing these words: 'She loves me.' Yes, child! I most certainly do. If I do nothing else right, I have shown one child that I love him.

Just as I work hard to connect with my students, God is always calling to us and reaching out to draw us into relationship. It can be difficult to feel God's pats on the back or hear God's whispers of encouragement. But when we take time to know God's character through reading scripture and observing creation, we grow closer to God. What joy it must bring God to hear us say, 'God loves me!'

Prayer: *Dear God, thank you for calling us into deeper relationship with you. Amen*

Thought for the day: God loves me!

Kami K. Preston (Tennessee, USA)

Promise fulfilled

Read Matthew 28:16–20

'I am with you always, to the very end of the age.'
Matthew 28:20 (NIV)

When my husband and I received an urgent message that my father was not doing well, we immediately bought plane tickets and flew to Buenos Aires. Two cousins met us upon arrival. I asked them which hospital my father was in, only to be told that he had died. As I tried to grasp the situation, the despair made it difficult to breathe. I thought, *My father is gone! I have no idea how I will live without him.*

I was with my mother when we arrived at the church for my father's funeral service. As we were walking in, I felt the warm touch of someone's hand on my arm. I turned, thinking it was my husband, but no one was there. I believe in my heart that it was Jesus Christ taking me by the arm, giving me strength for the coming days. I don't remember the rest of the time during the visitation, only that warm touch and the feeling of comfort, love and support it gave me.

Each time I remember that moment, I acknowledge the reality of today's scripture. The Lord fulfilled that promise to me and never left my side.

Prayer: *Merciful God, when our spirits are crushed, remain with us and sustain us. Thank you for the constancy of your love. In the name of Jesus we pray. Amen*

Thought for the day: God is with us always – in seasons of grief and in times of joy.

Neri Ruth Gattinoni (Chubut, Argentina)

Beautiful melodies

Read Psalm 96:1–3

'No one pours new wine into old wineskins. Otherwise, the wine will burst the skins, and both the wine and the wineskins will be ruined. No, they pour new wine into new wineskins.'
Mark 2:22 (NIV)

I have been playing the guitar for more than 50 years. I especially enjoy playing alone on a Sunday afternoon. It is almost like praying with my fingers. But every three months or so, no matter how much I tune them, the strings begin to sound tired and flat. Then I must do one of my least favourite tasks: change the guitar strings. I slowly unwind and throw away the old strings. I painstakingly tighten the new ones to their proper tension, adjusting them until they are properly tuned. It's a lot of trouble, but with new strings even the plainest melody rings with beauty.

I have discovered that sometimes God works in me the same way. When my life has gotten out of tune, God sits me down and starts changing my strings. God unwinds my attitudes and goals that have a selfish sharp sound and gently leads me to repentance. Next, God puts on the new strings, tightening them until the grace notes of Jesus Christ can be heard again in my heart. When the Great Musician sits down to play the beautiful melodies of life in me again – oh, what joy!

Prayer: *Father God, forgive us when our decisions do not follow your will. Tune our hearts to sing the songs of heaven today. Amen*

Thought for the day: Today I will sing a new song to the Lord.

Peter Caligiuri (Florida, USA)

My focus

Read Philippians 4:4–9

Whatever is true, whatever is honourable, whatever is just, whatever is pure, whatever is pleasing, whatever is commendable, if there is any excellence and if there is anything worthy of praise, think about these things.
Philippians 4:8 (NRSV)

Some days everything seems wrong, and everywhere I go appears dismal. I notice dirt on the floor, smudges on the windowpanes, a new grey hair and an endless list of stressors. While driving, traffic lights take too long to change, drivers are aggressive and I have to avoid potholes.

When I meditate on today's scripture verse, I realise that the real problem may be my focus. If I focus on what's wrong, that's what I'll see. But if I focus on what is lovely, pure and just, that's what I'll find. The world is full of both good and bad, and God tells us to meditate on and fill our hearts and minds with the good. In this way we can exhibit the peace that draws others to Christ.

When we change our focus, we are sure to find God in every part of creation. When I notice the amazing aroma of coffee, the birdsong outside my window or the stunning colours of a sunrise, my problems fade into the background. When my day is interrupted, I can pause to enjoy a few deep breaths and remind myself of my blessings. May we focus on what is lovely, pure and just as we observe the world around us today.

Prayer: *Dear God, help us to shift our focus away from what is stressful to see what is lovely in the world you have created. Amen*

Thought for the day: Today I will seek God's presence everywhere I go.

Melanie Sue Fretz (Pennsylvania, USA)

Joy in sacrifice

Read Matthew 19:23–30

'Everyone who has left houses or brothers or sisters or father or mother or children or fields, for my name's sake, will receive a hundredfold, and will inherit eternal life.'
Matthew 19:29 (NRSV)

In summer 2011, I was in Singapore for what I thought would be a short trip to renew my visa before returning to my mission field in northern India. I was excited to email my sponsoring church and report on my first few months' work, but I was distraught to learn they would not be sending the funds necessary for me to continue missionary service. I came to the painful conclusion that my missionary dreams in India were over.

I had left a trunk in India filled with everything I owned. Now, all my earthly possessions fit in a school bag. I quit mission work and went to Korea, feeling dejected. I was just trying to serve God. Why didn't God provide?

From today's scripture, we learn that serving God can come with the loss of comfort, security and even future prospects. At the same time, I have learned much from my many and varied experiences. I have gained friends and family; I've lived in several countries without ever lacking shelter, food or the sweet fellowship of God's people.

When we make sacrifices for God, we gain more than we can imagine, both in this life and most certainly in the life to come.

Prayer: *Dear God, give us courage to risk our own comfort so that we can lead others to know the joy that you alone can give. Amen*

Thought for the day: Making sacrifices allows me to serve God more fully.

Dennis Oh (Ho Chi Minh City, Vietnam)

Free from fear

Read John 8:31–32

'You will know the truth, and the truth will make you free.'
John 8:32 (NRSV)

I cried for the first five years of my daughter's life. She had been alive for only eight months when she was diagnosed with Williams Syndrome, a rare genetic disorder characterised by growth delays. Though not life-threatening, the disorder can manifest in a spectrum of symptoms that range in severity. Her unknown future was extremely frightening for me.

At first, I let my fears overwhelm me. Lies and assumptions took root in my mind and grew ferociously. Our new reality was choking me even though I claimed to trust God. Finally, a Bible study at church showed me how to counteract my fears with the truth of God's word. I listed all the lies I had been listening to and then replaced them with the truth. For example, when I wrote, 'The future is too overwhelming to think about,' God led me to Jeremiah 29:11. Or when I worried that I wouldn't be able to be a good enough parent, this fear was answered by 2 Corinthians 12:9.

As I meditated on these truths my fears diminished. As I continued to study more of the Bible, God's word gave me not only freedom from fear but also perspective and hope. We don't have to let fear consume us. When we put our fears into words, God's word answers us with truth and hope.

Prayer: *Dear God, by your grace open our eyes to what is true. Give us hope as we look to the future. Amen*

Thought for the day: God's truth can free me from fear.

Cheryl Esper Balcom (Michigan, USA)

PRAYER FOCUS: CHILDREN WITH RARE GENETIC DISORDERS

Follow in his footsteps

Read Matthew 4:18–22

'Come, follow me,' [Jesus] said.
Matthew 4:19 (CEB)

I live near the ocean, and I love to walk on the beach. Experiencing the changing seasons and feeling the sand go from frozen and snowy to scorching hot causes me to reflect on the seasons of life.

When my granddaughter Kacey visits on summer weekends, we often go to the beach. We load our items into a beach cart and eagerly begin our journey. Pulling the cart downhill to the water is no problem for Kacey. But on the way back, the cart feels heavier, and the sun and sand seem hotter. She struggles to walk in the shifting sand and pull the cart uphill. I advise her to step in the existing footprints in the sand because someone has previously packed that sand and created a foundation for her to follow.

Just as Jesus called his disciples as he walked along the beach, he also calls us to follow in his footsteps. Jesus guides us through challenges and situations because he has already been there. He knows what we're experiencing and wants to lighten our burden. Even when we don't know exactly where we're going or how we'll get there, we can trust that Jesus knows and will love us every step of the way.

Prayer: *Loving Saviour, thank you for leading us through life's challenges and for loving and empowering us each step of the way. Amen*

Thought for the day: Jesus guides my way when I prayerfully trust his guidance.

Connie Paulson (Delaware, USA)

Remembering promises

Read Hosea 6:1–3

So do not fear, for I am with you; do not be dismayed, for I am your God. I will strengthen you and help you; I will uphold you with my righteous right hand.
Isaiah 41:10 (NIV)

I graduated from high school in June 2019 with nearly perfect grades. I hoped to attend law school at a prestigious university in Zimbabwe, but that didn't happen. I applied to two universities and was declined by one and told by the other that I would only be accepted to university if I stopped applying to law school. I was devastated and asked, *Why me?* Suddenly, all my wrongdoings and sins rushed into my mind. I told myself I was being punished.

I was mad at myself and at God. I asked, 'Aren't you supposed to be forgiving?' and 'Couldn't you punish me in any other way?' It took seven months before I was able to pray or open the Bible to seek answers. But when I did, God was there, telling me to trust and that everything would be okay.

My story does not have a miraculous ending right now, but it has a beautiful reunion between me and God as I remember that God's word has never failed and God's promises remain the same. I want to tell everyone who has distanced themselves from God that when they return to God's presence and promises, they will find understanding and peace.

Prayer: *Faithful God, thank you for loving us when we distance ourselves from you. Remind us that no matter our circumstances, we can find peace in your presence. Amen*

Thought for the day: Even when my life does not go as I had hoped, God's promises remain true.

Audrey Tafadzwa Chidavaenzi (Midlands, Zimbabwe)

Source of light

Read Job 9:1–10

'In the same way, let your light shine before people, so they can see the good things you do and praise your Father who is in heaven.'
Matthew 5:16 (CEB)

On a clear night I took our dog outside. The sky was beautiful. I often feel a sense of awe for God's creation, particularly when many stars and planets are visible in the night sky. How vast it is! I also feel a connection with Job who marvelled at the constellations of Orion and the Great Bear, all of which I can see thousands of years after Job did.

Another feature of the night sky that amazes me is that the objects that appear the brightest – the moon and some of the planets, like Venus and Jupiter – do not produce their own light. Unlike the numerous stars that generate their own light, the moon and visible planets have no intrinsic light of their own. Instead they reflect light from the sun.

In a similar manner, we shine the brightest when we reflect the light of God. If we will allow the Holy Spirit to help us stay attuned to God and to Jesus Christ, we will be better able to reflect that light to others. Even when things all around us seem dark, God and God's Son are an incredible source of light for humankind.

Prayer: *Creator of our vast universe, help us to remember that you are the source of light for our lives. Amen*

Thought for the day: The light of Jesus is brighter than any light of my own.

Douglas 'Rusty' Brown (South Carolina, USA)

Pea-soup fog

Read Isaiah 30:19–21

Whether you turn to the right or to the left, your ears will hear a voice behind you, saying, 'This is the way; walk in it.'
Isaiah 30:21 (NIV)

A number of years ago I went away to a reunion. To get to the place we were staying was quite a trek and the route included a few different motorways. I was travelling alone at night and entered an area of thick fog, and the traffic slowed to a crawl. The only things visible were the fog lights of the other cars.

When I left the motorway, the fog intensified and visibility was terrible. I didn't know where I was going and felt quite scared, a bit trapped and a long way from home. Then a voice spoke clearly giving me firm instructions on which way to turn and when – the satnav! The voice was very comforting and reassuring. I reached my destination, relieved.

It struck me that often in life we face circumstances that are like a pea-soup fog. We can't see a way through or what steps to take, and we get scared. But just as my satnav spoke clearly and gave me directions, Isaiah reminds us that God too can guide us, telling us which way to walk and what path to take. That guidance might come through our praying, as we read the Bible, from listening to a podcast or sermon, or from the advice of a trusted friend. However difficult and dense a situation we face, God is always there.

Prayer: *Dear Father, thank you for always being a guide through all that we face. Help us to listen. Amen*

Thought for the day: Today, I will listen to the voice of the Lord.

Caroline Mansell (England, United Kingdom)

Carrying a heavy load

Read Colossians 3:12–17

'My yoke is easy, and my burden is light.'
Matthew 11:30 (NRSV)

I phoned a friend whose husband suffers from multiple sclerosis. She herself does not enjoy the best of health. 'How are you today?' I asked. 'Well,' she replied, 'it's like I'm carrying a heavy suitcase around with me everywhere today.' We talked for a while, and at the end of our conversation she told me that she was feeling better. Being able to share her troubles with a friend had helped.

There are times when we all feel overburdened and would like to share that weight with someone. As Christians, we do indeed have someone: Jesus is only a prayer away! Jesus has assured us that we can bring our heavy burdens to him and find rest. As Christians, we can reach out to others with the love of Christ, sharing their burdens and lightening the load even as Christ does this for us. When we walk together with Christ, our burden is light.

Prayer: *Dear Lord, when we feel overburdened, help us to remember that you are only a prayer away. Remind us to share this knowledge with others. We pray as Jesus taught us, 'Our Father in heaven, hallowed be your name, your kingdom come, your will be done, on earth as it is in heaven. Give us today our daily bread. And forgive us our debts, as we also have forgiven our debtors. And lead us not into temptation, but deliver us from the evil one' (Matthew 6:9–13, NIV). Amen*

Thought for the day: How is God calling me to help lighten someone's burden today?

Bill Findlay (Scotland, United Kingdom)

Carefully shaped

Read Jeremiah 18:1–10

I went down to the potter's house, and I saw him working at the wheel. But the pot he was shaping from the clay was marred in his hands; so the potter formed it into another pot, shaping it as seemed best to him.

Jeremiah 18:3–4 (NIV)

My neighbour has a beautiful tree, a spreading green canopy with a gentle shape. Its loveliness is no surprise because my neighbour is fully dedicated to caring for and shaping her tree. I have watched her gently clip any wayward tangled leaf or stem, choosing what cut will make the best shape. After a battering storm she vigorously prunes the broken or damaged branches. Watching this process for several years, I have realised it holds a significant spiritual lesson: God shapes our imperfect lives.

Just as my neighbour shapes her tree, God is moulding me through everyday circumstances. God can use even shattering storms to do good work in me. I have experienced deep, devastating sorrow that ripped everything from me until all I could cling to was the simple belief that 'Jesus loves me, this I know!' Through these crushing times I often wondered, *How could all these difficult things possibly be working together for my good?*

I am learning to trust that God is dedicated to forming me into a better version of myself. My neighbour's tree is a beautiful reminder that God is carefully shaping me.

Prayer: *Thank you, Creator, for knowing just where we need your love to reshape our lives. Make us ready to do your work in the world. Amen*

Thought for the day: God is reshaping my life day by day.

Beverly Taylor (Arizona, USA)

Healing work

Read Revelation 21:1–5

Our citizenship is in heaven. And we eagerly await a Saviour from there, the Lord Jesus Christ, who, by the power that enables him to bring everything under his control, will transform our lowly bodies so that they will be like his glorious body.
Philippians 3:20–21 (NIV)

In 2020, I had basal cancer cells surgically removed from my face. To shrink and flatten the visible scar, I had to massage it several times a day. I also had to wear a medical silicone sheet over the scar for 23 hours a day. In other words, removing the scar required effort from me.

This experience led me to think about the varied scars we have in our lives. Some scars are visible, but most I believe are not – scars from abandonment, abuse, regrets from poor choices or disobedience to God's word. I'm thankful for doctors who can remove bad cells or counsellors who can help us uncover pain deep inside us. But I am most thankful that our Lord has already done the work of healing scars of spiritual separation. I can't work hard or long enough to heal myself or to earn my way into God's presence. Jesus, thankfully, did that work on the cross, offering forgiveness for our sins and healing our scars.

Some scars will always be part of us. But God promises that those who love and believe in Christ will receive a new body in heaven – where our scars, be they visible or invisible, will be no more (see Revelation 21:4). What an amazing promise!

Prayer: *Dear Lord, help us to cast our cares and fears on you. We trust you to sustain us until the day we are in your eternal presence. Amen*

Thought for the day: That which cannot be healed on earth will be forever healed in heaven.

Larry Scanlan (Maryland, USA)

Waiting faithfully

Read Proverbs 3:5–8

Wait on the Lord: be of good courage, and he shall strengthen thine heart: wait, I say, on the Lord.
Psalm 27:14 (KJV)

A heavy rain began to fall while I was on my way to work. I took cover and watched the other people moving hurriedly down the street, trying unsuccessfully to keep dry.

While I waited, I thought about how we are often like those people rushing through the rain. Impatient and desiring quick solutions, we ask God for help but often do not wait for an answer. We continue in the rain and feel frustrated about getting wet.

Soon the rain stopped, and I was able to go calmly on my way. In the same spirit, may we learn to wait in faith for the rain to pass. Putting our trust in God sometimes means waiting when we would rather take action. But waiting for God's guidance and help allows us to take shelter until the path ahead is clear.

Prayer: *Even when we are in a hurry, beloved Father, give us the patience to wait for your answer. In the name of Jesus Christ. Amen*

Thought for the day: If I wait, God will answer.

Denise Leite (São Paulo, Brazil)

My true identity

Read Colossians 3:1–4

I have been crucified with Christ and I no longer live, but Christ lives in me. The life I now live in the body, I live by faith in the Son of God, who loved me and gave himself for me.
Galatians 2:20 (NIV)

One of my biggest struggles in my teenage years was comparing myself to others and trying to meet the world's standards for beauty, knowledge and skill. I thought my identity was in my looks, what others thought of me, how many friends I had and my achievements.

It is easy to fall into a cycle of comparison and insecurity. But as I got older and grew in my faith, I realised that those worldly standards don't have eternal meaning. Being brought up in a Christ-centred atmosphere, I was constantly reminded that, as God's daughter, I don't need to try to be anyone else. I am amazing as I am.

I am now entering a new chapter of my life and beginning university. I still struggle with comparing myself to others and worrying what people think of me, but I remind myself that it only matters what God thinks of me. Growing in my relationship with Jesus Christ and sharing Christ's love with others is what truly matters.

Prayer: *Dear God, help each of us to find our identity in you and keep our minds focused on things above. Amen*

Thought for the day: I am amazing because I am God's beautiful handiwork.

Emily Morren (Texas, USA)

Light from a cross

Read John 8:12–19

When Jesus spoke again to the people, he said, 'I am the light of the world. Whoever follows me will never walk in darkness, but will have the light of life.'
John 8:12 (NIV)

It is Christmas Day 2020, and I'm sitting in my friend's living room in Tønsberg, Norway, looking at the old watchtower on top of Fortress Hill. Churches are closed because of the Covid-19 pandemic. I have not seen my children and grandchildren since March, and I feel lonely and sorry for myself – in spite of being with my friend.

To my surprise, I notice that on top of the tower is a large cross spreading its light over all the town. I sense new feelings within me, as if my gloomy thoughts and self-pity must yield to the light from the cross.

Jesus told us that he is the light of the world. And in this moment it is as if Jesus is assuring me, 'You are never alone as long as I am with you, and I have not and will never forsake you. Darkness will give way to dawn. Wait and see.' I rest my eyes on the cross that shines not only over the town but in my heart as well – and I am comforted.

Prayer: *Dear God, thank you for your light in the world and in our lives. Thank you for your love that never leaves us alone. Amen*

Thought for the day: The light of Christ is stronger than my loneliness.

Øystein Brinch (Oslo, Norway)

PRAYER FOCUS: THOSE ISOLATED FROM FAMILY AND FRIENDS

Face to face

Read 2 Corinthians 3:12–18

God raised us up with Christ and seated us with him in the heavenly realms in Christ Jesus.
Ephesians 2:6 (NIV)

My friend Sarah was overjoyed to have been able to get a ticket to a classical concert at the Royal Festival Hall at the last minute. She was somewhat embarrassed, however, when she found her seat was in the stalls behind the orchestra, in view of audience members in their expensive seats and finery.

Once the conductor stepped up to the podium, however, she realised that God had given her a special blessing. Had she sat in a more expensive seat, my friend would only have seen the conductor's back. But from where she sat, Sarah could see the conductor's face. She was able to not only enjoy the music, but also share in the conductor's expressions of rapture and joy as he called in each section of the orchestra in turn.

As Sarah shared her experience with me, I realised how blessed we are being seated with Christ in the heavenly realms, so that we are able to, as it were, look upon the face of the creator God, who has before him the score for the whole drama of creation's symphony. We may not understand many of the discords and clashes, but we can look into his face and find there joy, peace and assurance that everything is under his control.

Prayer: *Dear Lord, may you, in the words of the ancient priestly blessing, make your face shine upon us and be gracious to us (see Numbers 6:24). Amen*

Thought for the day: The Lord turns his face towards me.

Pauline Lewis (Wales, England)

Psalms

Read Psalm 3

I have trusted in your faithful love. My heart will rejoice in your salvation.
Psalm 13:5 (CEB)

Often I do not know how to pray. Usually my prayers are check-the-box requests delivered in a steady, professional manner. The psalms show a different way of praying that is eloquent, raw and emotional. They pull us in deeply to what the writer was thinking or feeling. In many of the psalms the author shares feelings – good and bad, uplifting and disturbing, but always honest.

Though about one third of the psalms are laments, almost every one ends on a positive note. This encourages me always to try to end my prayers on a positive note. But if I cannot, if I am feeling too broken, confused or crushed, then it is okay to end where I am. I am confident that God would rather hear an honest prayer that does not end on a high note than one that is falsely hopeful.

The psalms teach us how to talk to God – to give God not only our requests but also our emotions. Prayers do not have to be as eloquent as the psalms. They just have to be honest and heartfelt.

Prayer: *O God, we offer our whole hearts to you. Thank you for loving us just as we are. Amen*

Thought for the day: Today I will pour out my heart to God.

Bob LaForge (New Jersey, USA)

By grace

Read Colossians 1:9–14

We continually ask God to fill you with the knowledge of his will through all the wisdom and understanding that the Spirit gives, so that you may live a life worthy of the Lord and please him in every way.

Colossians 1:9–10 (NIV)

In 2019, I had the opportunity to teach a creative writing course for a group of accomplished expatriates who wanted to write about their experiences living in a foreign land. I didn't know about the course until a few weeks before the start date, and I had not applied for the position. However, the programme director called and asked me if I was interested in teaching the course. He and I had previously worked together, and he trusted my ability. He hoped I would accept the opportunity.

At first, I felt unfit and undeserving of the job. Was I qualified? Would I be able to stand before these important people? But it was a privilege to have been specially chosen, and that meant I had as much right to teach the course as anyone.

This reminds me of what God, through Jesus, has done for us. We are not worthy of God's grace or forgiveness. God chooses us, freely gives us the gift of grace, and offers us the right to be children of God! Let us remain assured that by grace we are worthy of all that God has called us to do.

Prayer: *Dear God, sometimes we feel small, weak and unworthy. Help us to remember that through your Son, Jesus, we are worthy. Amen*

Thought for the day: Because God has called me, I am worthy.

Adhiambo E. Ochien'g (Nairobi, Kenya)

God of all comfort

Read 2 Corinthians 1:3–7

Praise be to the God and Father of our Lord Jesus Christ, the Father of compassion and the God of all comfort.
2 Corinthians 1:3 (NIV)

My first chemotherapy session took 10 hours in a room with about 20 other patients. In addition to the comfort my faith gave me, the kindness the other patients showed me on that first day was a real lesson in the fruit of the Spirit.

One woman, Linda, had been fighting cancer for a long time. When a nurse came to explain that her therapy had not been approved and that she would have to come back yet another day, Linda gave the nurse an exhausted smile. With kindness and patience Linda said, 'I understand. Things happen.' Linda gathered her blanket and cane, preparing to leave. As she passed me, something – maybe the fear on my face – led her to come over and give me the bracelet she was wearing. She said, 'I hope these two verses, 2 Corinthians 1:3–4, comfort you as they have me.'

While spending time in the hospital, doctors' offices, treatment centres, operating rooms and my home, I could look back and see Linda's face as she gifted me with scripture. Though she had surely suffered much, she took the time to reach out and comfort me. I never saw Linda again, but I felt the need to share her story and the gift of comfort God gave me through her.

Prayer: *Dear Lord, thank you for the people you send to us in our times of need and for the comfort they offer. May we, in turn, be faithful to comfort others. In Jesus' name. Amen*

Thought for the day: Because God comforts me, I can comfort others.

Martha J. Morris (Tennessee, USA)

Love brings freedom

Read Psalm 103:1–5

But I, by your great love, can come into your house.
Psalm 5:7 (NIV)

I am a singer and songwriter and have written and performed many songs over the years. I wrote my most recent song for my wife, and it opens with the lyric, 'When you told me that you loved me, you set my heart free.' I have always said that I was not fully myself until I met the woman who was to become my wife. Loving her set me free from the longing and loneliness I had felt for years.

Now I realise that this is also true about my relationship with God. I tend to be keenly aware of my failures and to feel that I am somehow not worthy of love. But God's love is unconditional and complete. God knows all my failures, and God loves me truly and completely in spite of myself. This knowledge has set me free to love and to be loved in Christ. I am no longer focused on my failures but on the redeeming power of God's love for us all. My love for my wife has helped me understand God's love for us. And love has given me the freedom to live fully in the grace of God. God's desire for us is to live abundantly joyful lives.

Prayer: *Holy and loving God, free us to live as your beloved children, eager to do your will. Amen*

Thought for the day: God's love sets me free.

Michael Albanese (New York, USA)

Falling leaves

Read Matthew 6:25–34

*'Do not worry about tomorrow, for tomorrow will worry about itself.
Each day has enough trouble of its own.'*
Matthew 6:34 (NIV)

For years I lived in a second-floor apartment. When I moved into a house, I began the daily task of sweeping leaves in front of the house and the back patio. It seemed a never-ending task! There were always leaves on the ground the following day. At first I tried shaking the tree limbs to make more leaves drop in hopes that there would be few or no leaves to sweep the next day. But the next day, there were always leaves on the ground.

Much like this task of sweeping up the leaves, when I face difficult tasks or physical challenges, I want to deal with them all at once and free myself of the aggravation and stress. But, like the leaves, no matter how much I want to resolve situations in one fell swoop, each day brings its own set of worries. This reality has led me to depend more on the Lord.

Each day leaves will fall, and worries will come. Now, instead of complaining about sweeping up leaves or being consumed with worries, I seek joy in the spiritual practice of discernment, trusting in divine providence to be my guiding light in all circumstances.

Prayer: *Creator God, help us to learn to depend on you each day, knowing that you will guard our going out and coming in. In the name of Jesus. Amen*

Thought for the day: 'Do not fear, [the Lord] will help you' (Isaiah 41:13, NRSV).

Yessenia Rosalía Acosta de Beard (Dominican Republic)

Every step of the way

Read Romans 8:38-39

Be content with what you have, because God has said, 'Never will I leave you; never will I forsake you.'
Hebrews 13:5 (NIV)

After a long, hot summer, my family took a trip to the mountains to hike in the cool weather. My son planned our first hike, one that promised an amazing panoramic view at the top. Halfway up the trail, we stopped at a lovely overlook. As we ate our lunch, we enjoyed speaking with the hikers who passed us. Many remarked on the beautiful view at the top. After lunch we continued up the trail. But when we were a half mile from the summit, the rain came pouring down. My son suggested we keep climbing through the dense rain. But even if we reached the top, I gently explained, there would be nothing to see. The mountaintop was covered in clouds, and the view was gone. So we made our way back to our car. Though we did not reach the summit, we agreed that we had experienced an exciting adventure and had enjoyed meeting many travellers.

I compare this story to my own faith journey. I always strive to be at the top of the mountain. While I often fall very short of this aim, I have learned that God is always with me, and this inspires me to continue the journey. Despite setbacks, God's abiding love surrounds us. Even if we don't always get to the top, God walks with us every step of the way.

Prayer: *Dear God, help us to remember that wherever our path may take us, you walk beside us and guide us every step of the way. Amen*

Thought for the day: How can I walk with God today?

Gretchen Nelson (Florida, USA)

A way through

Read Exodus 14:19–31

Give thanks to the Lord… who divided the Red Sea in two, for his steadfast love endures forever.
Psalm 136:1, 13 (NRSV)

As the Israelites made their way to the promised land, they faced an obstacle at the Red Sea. But because of God's love and mercy for the Israelites, God parted the waters and made a way for them. The Israelites then courageously continued their journey.

I remember when I had a 'Red Sea' before me. God had led me to my work, which I was doing in a rented space. I worked there for many years, but then I faced financial challenges and struggled to pay the rent. Although I desired to continue the work, I could see no way to pay the rent. I thought of giving up, but God made a way for me. Unexpectedly, I met a woman who had an interest in the kind of work I was doing, and she offered me premises free of charge to continue the work. God parted the sea before me, and I am continuing with the work I am called to do.

As we seek to follow our callings, we all face obstacles – financial struggles, marital issues, illness, job stresses and more. When we encounter an obstacle, we can call on our merciful God who can make a way for us and help us to the other side.

Prayer: *Dear Lord, when we cannot see a way past our difficulties, help us to trust in you. In Jesus' name. Amen*

Thought for the day: When I don't know how I will get through, God makes a way.

Enid Adah Nyinomujuni (Dar es Salaam, Tanzania)

PRAYER FOCUS: SOMEONE STRUGGLING TO PAY FOR HOUSING

A three-foot tornado

Read Psalm 139:1–6

I ask that Christ will live in your hearts through faith. As a result of having strong roots in love, I ask that you'll have the power to grasp love's width and length, height and depth, together with all believers.
Ephesians 3:17–18 (CEB)

'He's a three-foot-tall tornado.' I seem to say that every time our two-year-old grandson comes over. He grabs things out of drawers, pulls things off shelves and throws almost everything he touches. The house is a wreck after each visit. But a broken trinket and a messy house are a small price to pay for the sheer joy of having this bundle of love around. I wouldn't trade it for anything in the world.

I can't help but think that's how God loves me – despite all the times I've done things I know God would not be pleased with. After all the times I've failed to listen to God, and even after I've missed opportunities to show love to others, God still draws me close and tells me how much I am loved. That love is unconditional. As hard as it is for me to understand or believe, I know God wouldn't trade me for anything in the world. If it's true for me, then it's certainly true for all God's children.

Prayer: *Father God, we know that the best way to show our love for you is to love others. Help us see people as you see them and to show them the same compassion, love and mercy that you pour upon us daily. Amen*

Thought for the day: God loves me completely.

Glenn Way (Tennessee, USA)

Invitation to rest

Read Mark 6:30–34

If an axe is dull and one doesn't sharpen it first, then one must exert more force. It's profitable to be skillful and wise.
Ecclesiastes 10:10 (CEB)

For 28 years, I was consumed by my career as a faculty member and department chair at a local university. As with most educators, my job didn't end when I left campus for the day. Although my husband encouraged me to take time for rest and renewal, I often worked late into the evening to prepare for the next day.

But at the start of my 29th year at the university, I was diagnosed with breast cancer. Rest was no longer optional. To ensure I had adequate strength to continue serving my students and colleagues, I became more intentional about setting aside time every day to engage in restful activities, including prayer and reading scripture. I found the daily act of resting in God's presence to be especially helpful in calming my mind, body and soul so that I could face the next challenge.

I imagine my experience with rest is similar to what the apostles must have experienced when Jesus invited them to rest after they returned from their travels. Sometimes we do not prioritise resting in God's presence until we experience a stressful life event. As painful as my cancer diagnosis was, it saved my life by teaching me how to rest.

Prayer: *Father God, thank you for calling us to rest in your presence, strengthening our minds, bodies and souls for all you would have us do. Amen*

Thought for the day: Learning to rest prepares me to serve God well.

Jennifer Hegeman (Missouri, USA)

Try again

Read Luke 18:1–8

My flesh and my heart may fail, but God is the strength of my heart and my portion forever.
Psalm 73:26 (NIV)

My son, David, is learning to walk. As he stood holding on to a chair, his mother walked past him onto the balcony. David let go of the chair and started walking towards her. He took two steps, but he fell on the third. He waited a moment, looking for someone to help him. When no one came, he stood up and took a few more steps before he fell again and began screaming. This time, his mother rushed over to pick him up.

This got me thinking: if babies were to stop trying again after they fell, nobody would ever learn to walk. This brought to mind the parable of the persistent widow. Though she was denied justice several times, she refused to give up and ultimately got what she desired.

In my journey of faith, I have fallen many times and become weary. But by God's grace, I have gotten up and continued. Persisting in faith despite difficulties is always worthwhile. No matter how often you fall, take courage, stand up and take another step.

Prayer: *Loving God, no matter the challenges we face, give us the strength to rise up again and persist in faith. In Jesus' name. Amen*

Thought for the day: When I want to give up, God gives me the strength to persist.

Zeph Dim (Lagos, Nigeria)

PRAYER FOCUS: FOR PERSISTENCE IN ADVERSITY

Giants in the land

Read Numbers 13:26–33

Caleb silenced the people before Moses and said, 'We should go up and take possession of the land, for we can certainly do it.'
Numbers 13:30 (NIV)

As I reflected on today's scripture reading, I realised that we can approach our problems in two ways: we can either compare ourselves to the problem or compare the problem to God. In the reading, twelve leaders of the Israelite community were sent to explore the land of Canaan that God had promised the Israelites. On their return, the Israelite spies described the giants they found in the land that flows with milk and honey. Ten of the spies said, 'We can't attack those people; they are stronger than we are' (Numbers 13:31). Assessing their chance at victory, they relied on human logic and strength rather than having faith in God's promise. When they compared themselves to giants, they were sure they would lose. Instead, Caleb and Joshua trusted God. Caleb said, 'We should go up and take possession of the land, for we can certainly do it.' They measured the giants against God.

We face many giants – problems, temptations and tests that are too big for us to defeat on our own. But even the biggest giants are puny when we measure them against God. This knowledge fills me with hope and encourages me to trust in God, because I know God will prevail.

Prayer: *Dear God, we put our trust in you. Remind us that nothing we experience in this life is too big for you to handle. Amen*

Thought for the day: God is bigger than any problem I face.

George T. Wilkerson (North Carolina, USA)

PRAYER FOCUS: SOMEONE FACING GIANT OBSTACLES

Ash Wednesday

Read John 10:11–18

'I give them eternal life, and they shall never perish; no one will snatch them out of my hand. My Father, who has given them to me, is greater than all; no one can snatch them out of my Father's hand. I and the Father are one.'

John 10:28–30 (NIV)

A friend of mine moved to another city, and I had not seen him in a long time. I learned from another friend that he was sick. So I sent him a Bible with John 10:28–30 written on the bookmark I slid inside.

Two weeks after I sent him the Bible, I received a reply: 'The Bible verses you sent made me cry. I have been living far from God for a long time, and my life has become a mess. But it turns out that God's hand was always open to me. I am the one who removed my hand. I want to go back to holding God's hand.'

I trust that God never leaves us even though we often turn away from God. Our world is uncertain. Riots, chaos, natural disasters, failure, bankruptcy and illness mean we have no guarantee of safety. But God's loving presence remains steadfast, and God's promise of salvation is unshakable. No matter how far we feel we are from God, we can trust that God is always ready to take our hand and offer us new life.

Prayer: *Dear God, thank you for always extending your hand to us. Give us courage to return to you. Amen*

Thought for the day: The world may change, but God's love never does.

Linda Chandra (Banten, Indonesia)

Community

Read Matthew 5:13–16

'You are the salt of the earth. But if the salt loses its saltiness, how can it be made salty again? It is no longer good for anything, except to be thrown out and trampled underfoot.'
Matthew 5:13 (NIV)

Growing up, I attended a large church that seemed like a thriving community with many opportunities. I had good friends at church and enjoyed the worship, but I was not maturing in my faith. I thought that my relationship with God was strong because I attended church and took notes on the sermons, but I was just going through the motions.

During my junior year of high school, my parents decided to join a new church that was forming in our city. Since I was nearing the end of high school, they let me choose whether I wanted to join them. I prayed about it and joined the new church even though I knew no one there except my parents. I had no idea that the people in this church would become my best friends and help me grow significantly in my faith.

At the new church I was challenged in many ways – in my faith, to make new friends and to share the gospel with people around me. I found a community that was serious about their faith and lived it boldly. Leaving the comfort of my childhood church allowed me opportunities to deepen my relationship with God.

Prayer: *Dear Lord, help us not to become complacent in our faith but to strive for a better relationship with you always. Amen*

Thought for the day: Living in community with other believers helps me grow in my faith.

Mary Anneliese Hill (Texas, USA)

Speak through me

Read Hebrews 12:1–3

Just as the rain and the snow come down from the sky and don't return there without watering the earth… so is my word that comes from my mouth; it does not return to me empty. Instead, it does what I want, and accomplishes what I intend.
Isaiah 55:10–11 (CEB)

This is the sixth devotional I have written for *The Upper Room*. The first three were rejected. It was not until the fourth that I received the much-anticipated email saying, 'Your meditation is being held for further consideration,' meaning it might actually be published. Some might ask why I continued to write and submit after three rejections. The answer is prayer and perseverance.

In order to write and submit a devotional, I must pray, study and read scripture. After my initial rejections, I still felt led to write more after I prayed about it. It came to me that sometimes God may be talking only to me as I write, and sometimes God may be trying to reach someone else through my writing. Whether God uses what I write to speak just to me or to speak through me to someone else, those words accomplish what God intends. I must continue to run each race set out before me; I must not be discouraged, and I must not give up (Hebrews 12:1–3).

Prayer, study and reading scripture are important every day in our lives. It is how God can communicate not only with us but also through us.

Prayer: *Dear Father, guide us so that we can be your face, hands and feet to others. Help us to finish each race set before us. Amen*

Thought for the day: Time spent with God is always well spent.

Kim Koratsky (Tennessee, USA)

The making of a pearl

Read 2 Corinthians 3:12–18

If anyone is in Christ, there is a new creation: everything old has passed away; see, everything has become new!
2 Corinthians 5:17 (NRSV)

I recently saw a news segment reporting the discovery of the world's largest pearl. For a pearl to form, an irritant – a parasite, fish scale or some other bit of rubbish – makes its way inside a mollusc's shell. The mollusc then secretes a substance that covers the irritant, layer after layer. These layers, which protect the mollusc from the irritant, eventually become hard and lustrous pearls. The enormous pearl I saw on the news must have thousands upon thousands of glistening layers.

Rubbish can enter our lives through dangerous habits, unhealthy relationships, self-doubt or complacency. We may even come to believe that these irritants define us – that it is impossible to change. As God's transforming love covers us in layer upon layer of mercy and grace, we are protected and renewed, and our lives are made beautiful.

Prayer: *Recreating God, help us to trust your transforming love to shape the pieces of our lives into something beautiful. As Jesus taught us, we pray, 'Our Father which art in heaven, Hallowed be thy name. Thy kingdom come, Thy will be done in earth, as it is in heaven. Give us this day our daily bread. And forgive us our debts, as we forgive our debtors. And lead us not into temptation, but deliver us from evil: For thine is the kingdom, and the power, and the glory, forever. Amen' (Matthew 6:9–13, KJV). Amen*

Thought for the day: God's mercy, grace and love transform me.

Lu Fullilove (Texas, USA)

First Sunday of Lent

Read Matthew 11:25–30

'Come to me, all you who are weary and burdened, and I will give you rest. Take my yoke upon you and learn from me, for I am gentle and humble in heart, and you will find rest for your souls.'
Matthew 11:28–29 (NIV)

In many overwhelming times of my life, I held on to this scripture. Each season was challenging in its own way, but the major reason I clung to this scripture was my past – a life I had lived, what I had done, what I had said, how I had hurt my loved ones.

Every time I was in a situation that reminded me of everything I had done in the past, I fell to my knees with tears flowing on my face. I called upon Jesus, and every single time he reminded me of his love and that he died for me not because I was perfect but because I needed a saviour.

During the season of Lent we remind ourselves of everything Jesus has done for us. We all have different burdens that take away our strength and make us weary. But when that burden brings us to our knees, we can release it at the feet of Jesus and be at rest.

Prayer: *Dear Jesus, thank you for your unending love for us. Help us to trust your love so that we can release our burdens and live abundantly with you. Amen*

Thought for the day: I will allow Christ to take my burden so that I can find rest.

R. J. (Mwanza, Tanzania)

Tuning in

Read John 10:1–5, 22–28

'My sheep hear my voice. I know them, and they follow me.'
John 10:27 (NRSV)

A common feature of radio shows is to have listeners call in and attempt to answer questions to win a prize. While often the questions are general in nature, sometimes they are about something that was said or a song that was played during the broadcast. In that case, listeners will only know the answer if they have stayed tuned in over the course of the programme, and if they have been paying attention. Not only so, but they also need to respond at the right time, by phoning in.

Similarly in our lives, we need our 'spiritual antennae' to be constantly attuned to the Lord's voice speaking to us and to be ready to obey his leading. Even while doing other things, it is possible to still be 'in tune' with and attentive to God.

Sometimes other things crowd out our times of listening to God and meditating on his word, and of praising him in song as well as word. There are things we do which are good in themselves, but they must not become more important than time spent with God.

Prayer: *Lord Jesus, please help us to listen for your voice daily and to follow your guidance, whether it be to do something or not to do it. You have the words of eternal life. Amen*

Thought for the day: Time spent listening to God is never time wasted.

Christine Hay (Scotland, United Kingdom)

Gratitude

Read Luke 17:11–19

*He fell on his face at Jesus' feet and thanked him. He was
a Samaritan.*
Luke 17:16 (CEB)

In today's scripture reading, ten men with a skin disease stood at a distance and 'raised their voices' to Jesus, crying out for mercy. At that time these people would have been made to live on the outskirts of the city because of their disease. When they heard the news that Jesus could heal the sick, they came to him. Jesus asked them to show themselves to the priests. On their way to the temple, all ten men were healed. But one man came back to thank Jesus. He fell at Jesus' feet, expressing his gratitude and praising God.

Inspired by this man who expressed gratitude, I try to give thanks to God for every blessing I have received – even the smallest ones. When I travel by bus from college back to my hostel, I start thanking God. There are times when I forget to give thanks, like the days when I fall sick or when I have examinations, yet those days never feel complete.

So often we are ready to do what God says, but we cannot hear God's word because we are far away. We fail to see the distance that is created by our lack of gratitude. To reduce the distance between God and us, we can start giving thanks. The more we give thanks the closer we get to God.

Prayer: *Dear God, we give thanks for each blessing you bestow. Help us to draw closer to you through expressions of gratitude. Amen*

Thought for the day: Gratitude brings me closer to God.

Reshmisadhana Y. R. (Tamil Nadu, India)

Breaking with routine

When I was four years old, my family went on holiday to the beach. We arrived, ate lunch and then headed out to play in the ocean. That evening, we gathered around the table for dinner. As we finished blessing the food, my mother looked at me only to see tears rolling down my cheeks. 'What's wrong?' she asked. 'Daddy is sitting in *my* seat!' I wailed. Sitting in a different chair for dinner was an unwelcome change. Our one previous meal had created a routine that, even as a young child, I expected and craved. There are still times, decades later, that I resonate strongly with my four-year-old self. I want to know what to expect and what is expected of me, and, most important, I want to feel prepared, especially if change is involved.

Creating and following a routine is one way I find security and comfort when parts of life feel out of control. My routines give me a place to start when the day feels overwhelming or the tasks ahead of me appear daunting. Routines can be life-giving. Daily Bible reading, meditation and prayer connect us with God and provide depth to our spiritual life. And my regular walks around the neighbourhood help me care for my body and offer me space to quiet my mind. But even good routines, if we never inspect them or break from them, may lose their purpose. And sometimes when we rely too heavily on a particular routine, we risk losing opportunities for surprise and wonder or we may miss out on the unexpected and unplanned ways that God is working in our lives.

In John 5, Jesus meets a man who has been ill for 38 years and has tried all that time to get to the freshly stirred, healing waters of the pool called Bethesda. Each time the waters are stirred and the man moves towards them, someone else reaches them first. He has tried for nearly four decades, doing the same thing over and over. Finally, Jesus asks him, 'Do you want to be made well?' The man replies, 'I have no one to put me into the pool' (John 5:6–7, NRSV). This suggests to me that perhaps the man's routine of trying to get to the water had become all-consuming, that he had lost sight of the real goal of being made well. Jesus' question interrupts his routine and points to the heart of the matter – healing. And at Jesus' instruction the man takes up his mat and walks.

Like the man in this story, my routines can become all-consuming. Marking items off my to-do list feels comforting and satisfies my need for stability. But following a routine for the sake of a routine offers nothing in the way of healing or life-giving energy. God is always at work – but sometimes not in ways we expect or in ways we have planned for. When Jesus asks the man, 'Do you want to be made well?' I imagine him thinking, *Of course! Can't you see how I have spent years trying to get to the healing waters?* Instead of helping him to the water, however, Jesus interrupts his routine and tells him to 'stand up, take your mat and walk'. And scripture says, 'At once the man was made well' (John 5:8–9). The routine was not the answer. Jesus invites the man to break from his routine and to be open to a different path to the miracle that he wanted.

What miracles – large and small – do we miss because we are committed to a routine that numbs our awareness of other possibilities? I pray that Jesus will interrupt our routines when they are stale and no longer life-giving and invite us in a new direction. In this season of Lent, let us step out of the routines that limit our expectations of what God can do in our lives and in the world so that we may live abundantly.

QUESTIONS FOR REFLECTION

1 Recall a time when a disruption gave you a clearer awareness of God's presence. What was the disruption? What did you learn about God from that experience?

2 Which of your routines have become more important than the purpose they were intended to serve?

3 How will you disrupt one of your routines to make room for the Holy Spirit to push you in a new direction?

Lindsay L. Gray, editorial director

Incredible faithfulness

Read Philippians 4:4–7

This is the confidence we have in approaching God: that if we ask anything according to his will, he hears us.
1 John 5:14 (NIV)

When I receive a new issue of *The Upper Room*, I turn to the first page and draw a large T, like an accountant would use for debits and credits. On the left side, I write down the list of prayers and petitions that I want to present to God. They often include such things as an elderly aunt in a nursing home; a family member starting a new job or school; or the tendonitis affecting my right elbow.

On the right side, I write some things I am thankful for. They may include recent prayers which have been answered: 'Thank you for a healthy newborn grandchild,' or 'Thank you for healing my wife's sprained ankle.' I also like to incorporate some long-standing blessings I have received from God through the years: 'Thank you for protecting our home and our family' or 'Thank you for loving, Christian parents who raised me.'

Each morning, after reading the meditation for the day, I review my list and follow Paul's admonition to present my prayers and petitions to God with thanksgiving. By the time I receive my next issue, I am often amazed at how many of my prayers and petitions have been moved to the thanksgiving side of the ledger. Tracking my prayers in this way has revealed to me the incredible faithfulness of God.

Prayer: *Thank you, Lord, for always hearing and answering our prayers, and for the many blessings you have given us. Amen*

Thought for the day: Today, I will turn over my fears and troubles to God.

Douglas L. McWhorter (Alabama, USA)

PRAYER FOCUS: THOSE SUFFERING FROM ANXIETY

Renewed in Christ

Read 2 Corinthians 4:7–18

We do not lose heart. Though outwardly we are wasting away, yet inwardly we are being renewed day by day.
2 Corinthians 4:16 (NIV)

My brother, a congressman and devoted public servant, suffered from Lewy body dementia. It was painful to watch the disease take my brother from me as his body and mind deteriorated year by year, month by month and sometimes day by day. Some days he could no longer remember who he had married or how old he was.

During this time, my brother was in a Bible study with two close friends who observed his decline. Near the end of his life, he had glimpses of heaven; he would talk to his deceased parents and grandparents and see light. In his final days, he assured his family that everything would be all right. As his body and mind approached their earthly end, my brother seemed to be at peace – a peace that surpassed understanding (see Philippians 4:7).

Today's scripture reading comforted me. Although my brother had been wasting away for a long time, in Christ his spirit was being made new each day. What a hopeful message for us all! As we age and our bodies begin to decline, the Bible assures us that 'we are being renewed, day by day,' until it is time for us to go home to our Lord and Saviour.

Prayer: *Loving God, even as our bodies fail us, comfort us with the knowledge that we are being renewed in spirit through the love of Christ. Amen*

Thought for the day: Even as my body declines, my spirit is made new in Christ.

Sheryl Ramstad (Minnesota, USA)

Our comforter

Read John 14:15–21

'I will pray the Father, and he shall give you another Comforter, that he may abide with you forever.'
John 14:16 (KJV)

I sat waiting to take my entrance exams for a second time. I had recently started seeking God's guidance again after many disappointments, and I felt excited because I knew I could ask God anything. I asked that the Holy Spirit would sit beside me, and immediately I knew that the Spirit was there helping me. That was the first step in refreshing my relationship with God.

God has given us the Holy Spirit as our comforter. But if we fail to recognise the Spirit dwelling with us and in us, we miss out on the comfort and company we have on our journey. In today's reading from John, Jesus explains that we can know and have a relationship with the Spirit. We do this through recognition of the Spirit's presence, along with consistent communication and fellowship. When we maintain our connection to the Spirit, we are better able to follow the Spirit's leading and power in our lives. It is a great joy to know the One who dwells within us.

Prayer: *Dear God, thank you for your presence in our lives through the Spirit. Help us to maintain our relationship with you no matter how busy we become. In Jesus' name. Amen*

Thought for the day: The Spirit of God comforts me and dwells within me.

Maudlyn O. Adeleke (Federal Capital Territory, Nigeria)

God waits patiently

Read 1 Corinthians 13:4–7

The Lord is waiting to be merciful to you, and will rise up to show you compassion. The Lord is a God of justice; happy are all who wait for him.
Isaiah 30:18 (CEB)

My two-year-old Australian Shepherd loves to play fetch. Over and over again she brings me the ball, or the frisbee, or the bone, or even the sock to throw for her. If I am busy, she patiently waits to get my attention. As soon as I put a book down, or an advert comes on TV, or I close the grill lid, she pops back up, dropping a toy at my feet for me to throw. She never grows tired of it.

This morning I am enjoying coffee in my study and trying to read my Bible as she yet again brings me the ball to throw down the hall. I tell her to leave me alone and return to my reading, which, ironically, is about God's patience – for which I am so grateful. It occurs to me that people continually bring all of their problems and worries to God who never, ever grows weary of us.

Even when we don't make the time, God is always present, lovingly waiting for our attention. God is great indeed!

Prayer: *Dear God, thank you for being patient with us, even when we are impatient with you. We pray as your Son taught us, 'Our Father which art in heaven, Hallowed be thy name. Thy kingdom come, Thy will be done in earth, as it is in heaven. Give us this day our daily bread. And forgive us our debts, as we forgive our debtors. And lead us not into temptation, but deliver us from evil: For thine is the kingdom, and the power, and the glory, forever. Amen' (Matthew 6:9–13, KJV).*

Thought for the day: God is patient with me, and I will be patient with others.

Jim Weems (Mississippi, USA)

Second Sunday of Lent

Read Romans 12:9–18
Love each other like the members of your family. Be the best at showing honour to each other.
Romans 12:10 (CEB)

When my husband was diagnosed with cancer last October, I was suddenly more aware of life's finite timeline. My husband's next breath wasn't guaranteed. But, then again, neither was mine.

Over the years, I have heard countless stories from friends and family who wished their last words with a loved one had been different. Some parted in disagreement, frustration or silence. Others spent a lifetime waiting to hear 'I love you' from a mother, father, grandparent or sibling.

With my husband's cancer diagnosis, I felt compelled to start saying 'I love you', not only to my family but also to my friends. Now I'm that friend who moves in first for the hug. I say, 'I love you', as I embrace them. I yell it across parking lots. I say it on the phone. I type it in texts. I never want my family and friends to wonder how I feel. Every chance I get I say, 'I love you.'

More important, I tell my friends and family that God loves them. I speak of God's mercy and grace. I give my testimony. I remind them that God is always good and that God is the reason that I end my conversations with 'I love you'.

Prayer: *Dear God, thank you for loving us and teaching us the importance of loving others. Amen*

Thought for the day: Because God loves me, I will never miss an opportunity to tell others I love them.

Christy Bass Adams (Florida, USA)

Filled up

Read John 4:7–14

'Whoever drinks from the water that I will give will never be thirsty again. The water that I give will become in those who drink it a spring of water that bubbles up into eternal life.'
John 4:14 (CEB)

Before I knew God, I thought I could fill the void within me through my achievements. I was sure that getting good grades in school, having wonderful friends, travelling, having a boyfriend or getting a job would finally solve everything. It was painful as each of these hopes failed to fill the emptiness I felt.

Eventually I accepted that it was irrational and cruel to expect humans to fulfil something that only God can. Accepting that we all have limitations is liberating and allows God's love to fill those spaces. Where our capabilities end, God's love stretches out to carry us.

Thankfully, God's love has filled the void that I felt. Now my joy and fulfilment are with me in the present rather than in the future, and I don't depend solely on my achievements, circumstances or loved ones. I can no longer imagine my life without God in it. And as I have grown in my faith, I have come to recognise God's presence throughout my life. God has always been faithful, even when I was not. Christ offers the water that will quench our thirst. And when we go to God with humble hearts, God will welcome us.

Prayer: *Faithful God, remind us that your love can fill the empty spaces in our lives. Amen*

Thought for the day: When I feel a void in my life, I will seek God's abundant love to fill it.

Rincy Mathew (Chhattisgarh, India)

First steps

Read Acts 3:1–10

Jumping up, he began to walk around. He entered the temple with them, walking, leaping and praising God.

Acts 3:8 (CEB)

Waking up in the early hours of the morning is hard for me. However, waking up in those early hours of the morning with a worshipping soul and a heart of praise is even harder. As a university student who is often up late, upon waking I usually think, *It is way too early for my day to begin.* That mindset made the mornings miserable. However, when I set my focus on God before I roll out of bed, those first steps of the day become more joyful.

The first steps of the man healed in Acts 3 were full of worship. Later in Acts 4:22, we see that the man was more than 40 years old. He had never taken a step in 40 years! He was healed by a miracle, and he praised Jesus as he began to walk.

Waking up every morning is a miracle in itself, and that's worth celebrating. Each new day is a gift from our gracious God.

Prayer: *Heavenly Father, thank you for the gift of your grace and for the gift of each new day. Help us to worship you and reflect your love with each step we take. In Jesus' name we pray. Amen*

Thought for the day: How will I give thanks to God for each new day?

Truman Culp (Texas, USA)

Important roles

Read Romans 16:1–15

I ask you also, my loyal companion, help these women, for they have struggled beside me in the work of the gospel, together with Clement and the rest of my co-workers, whose names are in the book of life.
Philippians 4:3 (NRSV)

Are you familiar with the names Jochebed, Shiphrah and Puah? I didn't readily recognise these names, but they were key players in Moses' birth story in Exodus 1. Jochebed was Moses' birth mother. Shiphrah and Puah were the midwives believed to have attended to his birth, also known to have defied the Pharaoh's order regarding newborn boys. Yet the names of these courageous women of God are not widely repeated or familiar. In today's scripture, the apostle Paul expressed his thanks to the church's faithful workers – many of them women whose names may not be familiar to us.

Likewise, we may not know the names of all the women who make our daily lives a bit easier. Today, on International Women's Day, let us take a moment to recognise the women who are there for us each day, such as customer service representatives, supermarket workers, bus drivers, postal workers, crossing guards, police officers and other first responders. They all play important roles in our lives and communities. Let us give them a heartfelt 'thank you' or a silent prayer of gratitude. We may not know their names, but let's never forget how important they are.

Prayer: *God of courage, thank you for all your workers here on earth. May we never take anyone for granted. Remind us to remain grateful, as Paul did, for the contributions of those around us. Amen*

Thought for the day: Every person is important to God.

Monica A. Andermann (New York, USA)

PRAYER FOCUS: WOMEN WHO MAKE A DIFFERENCE IN MY LIFE

'So help me, God'

Read Joshua 1:1–9

I call on you, my God, for you will answer me; turn your ear to me and hear my prayer.
Psalm 17:6 (NIV)

I have noticed a tradition in the United States where newly elected public officers swear an oath ending with the words, 'So help me, God.' How relevant those words are! These people are saying that they cannot carry out the tasks of their office without God's help.

I have followed the spirit of those words ever since I came to know that I am a child of God. Every time I embark on a task which looks difficult and daunting, I speak those words to God, and then proceed with the task confidently, knowing that God will help me to accomplish it. Joshua 1:9 says it clearly: 'Be strong and courageous. Do not be afraid; do not be discouraged, for the Lord your God will be with you wherever you go.' God encouraged Joshua to lead his people into the promised land. It was no easy task, but Joshua accomplished it with God's presence and power.

Whatever task we have before us – in our family, at work, in the community or at church – we can be assured that God is with us and will guide us. Psalm 17:6 says, 'I call on you, my God, for you will answer me.' When we pray and place our tasks into God's hands, we can complete our work trusting in God's help.

Prayer: *Heavenly Father, thank you for your constant presence with us. Help us look to you for help at all times. In Jesus' name, we pray. Amen*

Thought for the day: I will begin every task with prayer.

Kong Peng Sun (Singapore)

PRAYER FOCUS: NEWLY ELECTED PUBLIC OFFICIALS

The faith of children

Read Matthew 19:13-15

Jesus said, 'Let the little children come to me, and do not hinder them, for the kingdom of heaven belongs to such as these.'
Matthew 19:14 (NIV)

When I was young, my mother and I went to church only to attend the funerals of loved ones. I had little knowledge of Jesus. But that changed when I was five years old and Mama remarried. It was 1943, and my new dad was a soldier. We moved into an apartment near his military base, and things began to change for the better.

When our landlady invited us to her church, I wasn't thrilled. But I was in for a surprise when we visited for the first time. The people were warm and welcoming, and I loved the music. The songs about Jesus excited me. I soaked it all up and fell in love with Jesus.

The next day I found a pencil and paper and asked Mama how to spell 'Jesus.' I carefully wrote his name down and put the paper in my pocket. Every day I would turn the paper over in my hands, and I felt warmed and comforted. It eventually dissolved, worn out by those loving caresses.

I am now 83 years old and have seen many things dissolve. But I've learned that some things, like the love and comfort I still receive from Jesus, never go away.

Prayer: *Dear God, thank you for the people who have taught us about you and your son, Jesus. Remind us that no matter what we face, your love and presence remain steadfast. Amen*

Thought for the day: Though I will watch many things dissolve in life, Jesus will be with me always.

Jo Ann Johnson (Texas, USA)

Seeing in 3D

Read Hebrews 11:1–16
We live by faith, not by sight.
2 Corinthians 5:7 (NIV)

I remember the first time I saw a 3D picture in a poster shop that opened in our town. I stopped to look, but it seemed just like any other picture of a sea scene with corals and shoals of fish – nice and colourful, but hardly remarkable. When people around me started to 'Ooh' and 'Ah' at it, I knew I was missing something that they could see.

Over the next week I stopped to look again, but the picture remained the same, decidedly 2D image. Finally a lady told me to look into the picture beyond what I could see. As I let my eyes rest in the distance, I suddenly saw sharks and dolphins in relief in a 3D setting. They had been there all the time!

On reflection it struck me that this experience had been like my spiritual life. There were years in my late teens and early 20s when I drifted away from my faith and ceased to believe in God. I viewed the world in front of me as if that was all there is. When finally I turned back to God and recommitted my life to Jesus, it was as if I saw the world in all its multidimensional glory. As the writer to the Hebrews says, I now try to look beyond the world that I can see and long for 'a better country – a heavenly one' (Hebrews 11:16).

Prayer: *Dear Lord, may we help others to see you and find faith. Amen*

Thought for the day: Works of art can help me to experience God's loving presence.

Faith Ford (England, United Kingdom)

Third Sunday of Lent

Read Joshua 3:7–17

'Be strong and courageous. Do not be afraid; do not be discouraged, for the Lord your God will be with you wherever you go.'
Joshua 1:9 (NIV)

I stood staring at the far side of the 604-foot-long swinging pedestrian bridge that spanned a wide river far below. My fear of heights kept me rooted in place, unable to enjoy an adventure. My daughter promised not to make the bridge swing too much and encouraged me to face my fears by taking a few steps out on to the bridge. I hesitated a few minutes longer. The bridge appeared sturdy with thick, metal handrails. I watched someone stride across without pause or concern. The bridge swayed less than I expected.

One step at a time I began to move towards the other side. I paused in the middle to survey the wonderful view only visible from this new perspective. Then I completed my journey to the other side – one step at a time.

In Joshua 3, God commanded the Israelites to cross the Jordan River so they could enter the promised land. God instructed the priests to step into the river. They obeyed God's command to stand still in the raging flood waters before God miraculously stopped the river's flow and the people crossed on dry ground. We face many frightening moments, most of them beyond our control. Placing our trust in God helps us to conquer those fears and move forward.

Prayer: *Dear God, give us courage to face our fears and to trust that with your help, we can move forward – one step at a time. Amen*

Thought for the day: What fears do I need God to help me conquer today?

Carol Harrison (Saskatchewan, Canada)

How much is enough?

Read Matthew 14:15–21

A generous person will prosper; whoever refreshes others will be refreshed.
Proverbs 11:25 (NIV)

When my husband, Joe, and I were in our late 20s with a two-year-old daughter and a son on the way, Joe was fishing in a tournament. He noticed his right eye clouding, and he realised he needed medical attention. The diagnosis was a torn retina, and, under the care of a wonderful physician, Joe underwent many surgeries over the next two years. Ultimately his retina could not be repaired, and the vision in one eye was lost.

To thank the physician for his excellent care, we wanted to share some of our fish. I took a few packages from the freezer and placed them in a cooler. Later I was prompted to put in another package. The prompting continued until I said, 'Okay, Lord, I hear you. These are your fish; we were just lucky enough to catch them. If you want all the fish, nothing would please us more.' After all the fish were packed, a peace came over me and I knew the Lord was pleased.

How many fish were enough? By my standards, a few packages. By God's standards, the whole catch. In our relationships, family time, projects serving our community and church, God asks us to give 'the whole catch' in everything we do.

Prayer: *Generous God, thank you for continuing to teach us to give as you have given to us. Amen*

Thought for the day: When I think I have given enough, I still can give more.

Sandy Hall (Missouri, USA)

Our promise

Read Romans 8:31–39

Who shall separate us from the love of Christ? Shall trouble or hardship or persecution or famine or nakedness or danger or sword?
Romans 8:35 (NIV)

I was eager to speak with my family in Mexico by phone. I am currently in prison and have limited phone privileges. My wife was not available at the time of the call, but I talked with my parents, then my son and finally my daughter.

As I was talking to her, I detected something different in her tone of voice. Suddenly she started to cry and struggled to tell me that the fish I had given her for her birthday had died. I tried to console her and explain why that might have happened, but she didn't want to talk anymore. She simply said, 'Bye, Daddy. God take care of you.'

After the call, I returned to my cell. I was overcome with sadness because I love my daughter, and it broke my heart to hear her cry. As I started to read my Bible, I realised how fragile we all are. But at the same time, I am ever grateful for the promise referenced in Romans 8:38–39 that nothing can separate us from the love of God that is in Christ. We know God will always care for us – God's unconditional love is our bond and our promise.

Prayer: *Merciful God, when we cry out to you, reassure us of your promise that nothing will separate us from your incredible love. Amen*

Thought for the day: 'See what great love the Father has lavished on us, that we should be called children of God!' (1 John 3:1).

Camacho De La Luz Armando (Florida, USA)

Support one another

Read 1 John 3:16–24

Serve one another humbly in love.
Galatians 5:13 (NIV)

At our church in Lagos, Laity Week is a time for every parishioner to visit with the sick and suffering. We go in groups to spend time in hospitals, elder-care homes, hospices, prisons, orphanages and charitable organisations. We witness a sea of suffering humanity. We give our support by giving our time and collecting our resources to help each person who is suffering. What consolation it gives a lonely person to have the cheerful company of believers who bring the message of Christ's love in words and action!

Lent is the time to redouble our efforts to support one another. We devote extra time and effort to our families. We welcome new neighbours. We soothe those who are anxious. Putting more love into our work, we try to be more understanding of our co-workers.

During Lent we contemplate the face of Jesus in every face we see. We see Jesus in those who are heartbroken, despised, sorrowful or rejected. We offer our support and allow the Christ to work through us. As we open our hearts, we receive the grace to stand with our brothers and sisters and share their burdens – not just during Lent, but every day of our lives.

Prayer: *Merciful Father, fill our hearts with your love so that we can share it with all who are suffering. Amen*

Thought for the day: I will seek the face of Jesus in every person I meet today.

Nenye Andy-Eke (Lagos, Nigeria)

PRAYER FOCUS: PEOPLE RECEIVING HOSPICE CARE

By God's grace

Read Ephesians 1:3–10

[God] destined us for adoption as his children through Jesus Christ, according to the good pleasure of his will.
Ephesians 1:5 (NRSV)

Our family embraced adoption several years ago, not as a second-best solution but as God's plan for forming our family. Whether children have come into our homes through biological birth or adoption, love is what makes a family.

Our son, now 17 years old, came to our family on September 9, 2006. I became his father the first day I laid eyes on his little face in a picture. It is always such a joy to hear from my son's lips the words, 'Dad, I love you,' a vivid reminder of God's love for me.

One of my greatest fears as an adult was becoming a father, since I was a fatherless child myself. What kind of example or guidance would I give a child? It turned out that the shared experience of not having a biological father present in our lives created a stronger connection between my son and me. I can relate to so many of his questions and concerns.

God provided what I needed, and little by little all my fears melted away through love and patience. Being a father is an ongoing process of learning from new experiences and challenges, and I am not perfect. Every day I pray for God to help me be the best father I can be for my son, so that he will have the tools and the assurance that God is there for him too.

Prayer: *O Lord, be with children who are waiting for a loving home and with families waiting for a child to call their own. Amen*

Thought for the day: I am blessed to be part of God's family.

Migdiel E. Pérez (Tennessee, USA)

God's surprises

Read Matthew 6:8–15

'Your Father knows what you need before you ask him.'
Matthew 6:8 (NIV)

I studied Greek in my college years to fulfil a language requirement. I chose a biblical language because it would help me in understanding scripture. I enjoyed the classes as well as the chance to practise Greek with my classmates.

Years later, after an unsuccessful marriage and with five young children to support, I was looking for a job where I could work from home. Working from home was not common at that time. My mother was a medical transcriptionist, and I was good at typing. So I set out to learn medical terminology in order to establish a career. As I began, I was delighted to see that I already knew a lot of the terminology because the Greek roots were familiar to me. What a joy! In a time of insecurity, it felt like an affirmation from God when I realised I had been preparing for this new role without knowing it.

Now, as I walk through life's many twists and turns, I can trust God's purposes more easily. I trust that challenging times are part of a bigger, perhaps divine plan. Looking for God's surprises makes life's journey richer.

Prayer: *O God, help us remember the ways you have worked in our lives, and give us vision and wisdom to see what you are doing now. Amen*

Thought for the day: God is at work in all things.

Becky Sutherland (South Carolina, USA)

PRAYER FOCUS: SOMEONE LEARNING A NEW LANGUAGE

God who saves

Read Luke 19:1–10

'The Son of Man came to seek and to save the lost.'
Luke 19:10 (NIV)

In my work as a nurse, I was caring for an elderly, dying patient. He was a grumpy man who would curse those caring for him. One day we were by his bedside as his doctor came in. I had told the doctor about our patient's unhappiness, so he offered the man some medication to improve his mood. But he angrily refused to take it.

At mealtime I went back to feed him and said to him, 'Something is bothering you. Would you like to talk about it?' He replied, 'No! No use!' Then I found the courage to ask, 'May I pray for you?' His reply was even angrier: 'No!' I continued feeding him in silence. However, in my spirit I felt that the man regretted his abrupt reply.

The next morning, I returned to work and had to medicate him right away. He was deteriorating quickly, and he cried out, 'Help me.' I asked him, 'How can I help you?' He replied, 'Pray for me!'

I don't remember what I prayed. It felt a bit clumsy, but I trust God worked through that prayer. I never had another opportunity to pray with the man again. Later he slipped into unconsciousness and died.

I have continued to pray for my patients and to trust God to care for them too.

Prayer: *Thank you, God, for your amazing love and your gift of grace for us all. In Jesus' name. Amen*

Thought for the day: God loves to care for God's children.

Johanna (Finland)

Fourth Sunday of Lent

Read Acts 16:1–5

You then, my son, be strong in the grace that is in Christ Jesus.
2 Timothy 2:1 (NIV)

The life of the apostle Paul was a remarkable one – his dramatic conversion from a Pharisee who persecuted Christians to a leader of the early church; his many letters; his courage in the face of opposition; and most of all, his incredible faith in Jesus Christ. As he wrote in Philippians, 'To live is Christ and to die is gain' (Philippians 1:21).

I was part of a recent Bible study on Paul's letters to Timothy that revealed another attribute of his amazing life. From our discussion I gained a new appreciation for how Paul mentored his young companion. We can imagine all that Paul taught Timothy as they travelled together on several missionary trips. Then as Paul approached the end of his life, he put aside his own needs and took time to write letters of encouragement to Timothy, urging him to remain true to the gospel message that Paul lived to the fullest.

The story of Paul and Timothy is a good lesson for all of us. We all know younger people whom we can reach out to and mentor in the walk of faith. Paul's life is a great reminder to be more intentional about this opportunity, doing our part to encourage and equip others as they follow Christ.

Prayer: *Dear Father, thank you for the gift of your son, Jesus Christ. Help us to share this gift with others and to encourage them on their faith journey. Amen*

Thought for the day: Whom can I encourage in the walk of faith today?

John D. Bown (Minnesota, USA)

God gave me strength

Read Psalm 28:6–9

The Lord is my strength and my shield; my heart trusts in him, and he helps me.
Psalm 28:7 (NIV)

I was in my final year of university and about to present my thesis. I did not have a family member present because my grandfather, whom I had lived with for four years, was in poor health and several of my family members were caring for him.

While I was waiting among my schoolmates and their family members, my sister called and told me that our grandfather had died. I began to sob. Grief and worry for my family flooded my mind, and I was so over-whelmed that I collapsed and was taken to the infirmary.

My father called to tell me that if I chose not to present my thesis, he would support my decision. However, this would mean that the past academic year would have been wasted. The words of Philippians 4:13 came to me: 'I can do all this through him who gives me strength.' I centred my thoughts and asked God to help me. I was filled with a peace that I can't explain, and I decided to present my thesis.

Throughout the experience, I felt a deep connection to God, who provided the strength I needed. My friends, family and professors were astonished. I could only say: 'God gave me the strength.'

Prayer: *Eternal God, thank you for your abiding presence and for your word that reminds us to take heart and rely on you. Help us to seek you at all times and in all situations. In the name of Jesus. Amen*

Thought for the day: God is the true source of my strength.

Pilar González (Coquimbo, Chile)

Draw near

Read James 4:1–10

Draw near to God, and he will draw near to you.
James 4:8 (NRSV)

When I was a child I noticed that my parents and family members embraced, praised and sought after God only on major holidays or when hard times arose. We would go to church a couple of times each month, but there was a clear line between church life and home life; we rarely mixed the two.

As I got older, this practice didn't make sense to me. How could we treat the God who gives us life with such disregard that we come to him only on holidays or when we're in some kind of trouble?

As I have grown in my faith, I have learned an important lesson. The more time we give to God, the closer to God we become. God is worthy of all our attention, not just on certain days. The book of James says, 'Draw near to God, and he will draw near to you.' We don't need to wait until something goes wrong to seek God's presence. We can embrace God's presence in the good times and bad. True peace comes to us when we commit to staying near to God and God's way.

Prayer: *Dear Lord, in a world of distractions, keep our eyes open to find the true peace and security that come from you. Amen*

Thought for the day: In both good and bad times, I will draw close to God.

Zach Schaar (Ohio, USA)

Resilience and brokenness

Read Ecclesiastes 3:1–8

There is a time for everything, and a season for every activity under the heavens.
Ecclesiastes 3:1 (NIV)

In the winter I often walk through the woods with my dog. To make paths for us, sometimes I break off branches that are in the way. Most of them snap and easily break off, but some are so resilient that no matter what I do, they bend but don't break.

I used to think that I too should never break. I thought I should be so grounded in and sustained by my faith that in any circumstance, I could bend without breaking. But then in the spring, I witnessed the broken branches beautifully sprouting new growth. I realised that being resilient is worthwhile, but allowing myself to be broken could have its advantages too. Being pushed into new growth expands my perspective, possibilities and potential. When I let go of old patterns that no longer serve me, new patterns can take their place.

This has been a challenging year. While I have maintained an underlying resilience, I have also experienced moments of great brokenness. Being faithful doesn't always come with clear answers. Maybe there is a time to be resilient and a time to be broken. Perhaps we can embody both resilience and brokenness at the same time. Our spiritual journey just might require both.

Prayer: *Dear God, help us to welcome both resilience and brokenness. Create new growth in us so that we may reach our highest potential. Amen*

Thought for the day: Brokenness allows for new and beautiful growth.

Sue Konkel (Wisconsin, USA)

Called to write

Read Revelation 1:9–20

I heard behind me a loud voice that sounded like a trumpet. It said, 'Write down on a scroll whatever you see.'
Revelation 1:10–11 (CEB)

One afternoon I was feeling exhausted after the work of teaching primary school online from home during the pandemic. Suddenly, today's scripture verse echoed in my mind: *Write whatever you see.*

I didn't consider myself a writer, so I was particularly struck by this thought. I kept pondering the meaning of this verse, and deep inside, I felt that God was calling me to do something, but I didn't know what.

As I prayed and asked the Holy Spirit for guidance, I felt reassured. I shared my experience with my wife, and she encouraged me to obey God's call. So I did. I started by writing down my experience of following Jesus in a country where Christians are in the minority and shared my writing on my blog and with other publications. To my surprise, people started to read my words and told me they had been blessed by my writing.

From this experience, I have learned that the Holy Spirit can work in any situation. God will always find a way to spread the good news of Christ.

Prayer: *Dear Jesus, thank you for speaking to us and guiding us in the way we should go. Open our ears to hear your voice. Amen*

Thought for the day: What new ministry is God calling me to?

Ayub Simanjuntak (West Java, Indonesia)

God's good guidance

Read Isaiah 55:6–13

Your word is a lamp for my feet, a light on my path.
Psalm 119:105 (NIV)

As an attorney, my job often involves arguing my client's case before a judge. This requires a lot of time, preparation, thought and research. Sometimes the judge rules in my client's favour, but not always. It is disappointing when things don't go our way, but generally we must accept the judge's ruling.

I think it is easy for us to approach prayer like an argument before a judge. When we pray, we may try to give God reasons and explanations for why our prayers should be answered a certain way. But no matter how convincing we think our arguments are, if our desires don't line up with God's will, we are not likely to get the result that we want. While this may be discouraging for a time, we can trust that God's ways are higher than our ways. God has all the facts – many of which we may not be aware of. We can be assured that God's answers are always for our good. And when we trust God's direction, we will always find the right path.

Prayer: *Dear God, thank you for your guidance. Help us trust you to lead us to the path you have prepared for us. Amen*

Thought for the day: I can trust that God's answers to my prayers will lead me on the right path.

Valerie Hays (Oklahoma, USA)

Finding encouragement

Read Jeremiah 18:1–5

The vessel he was making of clay was spoiled in the potter's hand, and he reworked it into another vessel, as seemed good to him.
Jeremiah 18:4 (NRSV)

I was brought up in a Jewish home, but on Easter Sunday when I was 50 years old, I was baptised. The Holy Spirit entered my life, and I became a new Christian.

One day I went to my favourite café and found *The Upper Room* on the table. I read every story for the next month. I knew the Lord intended for me to find it, and it encouraged my new walk with Christ and my thirst for understanding.

Eleven years later, a friend and I were walking around a nearby university campus and found a small chapel. *The Upper Room* was on a table inside. I instantly remembered it and told my friend about my first copy. I took one home. As I read the real-life stories from people around the world who have a special relationship with Jesus, I was united with the writers.

Over time, I came to realise that I do not have to give up my Jewish traditions to have a relationship with Christ. Walking side by side with Christ has helped me find inner peace and also peace in my relationships. And the Lord brought the stories in *The Upper Room* into my life at just the right moment.

Prayer: *Dear Lord, thank you for the people and stories that encourage our faith. Help us to follow the path towards love that you have laid out for us. Amen*

Thought for the day: Every day I will look for the miracles that the Lord sends my way.

Claudia Merle Hochberg (Texas, USA)

Fifth Sunday of Lent

Read Colossians 3:1–4

We fix our eyes not on what is seen, but on what is unseen, since what is seen is temporary, but what is unseen is eternal.
2 Corinthians 4:18 (NIV)

Our deck was damaged in 2020 by the strongest typhoon on record at that time. After the storm, I tried to use a hammer and nails to repair it. But I wasn't strong enough and the nails still stuck out from the boards. My dad took over and drove the nails all the way in. As I watched him work, I asked why it was so important to ensure the nails were completely hammered in. He reminded me of how the second most powerful typhoon in the world had blown through seven years before. This stressed the importance of securely fastening the boards since more storms would likely come our way.

When Paul said to fix our eyes not on what is seen but on what is unseen, he understood how easily we can shift our focus to the temporal distractions around us. When we become distracted, we are like loose boards, unable to withstand the storm. When we firmly fix our eyes on the Lord, as securely as a nailed-down board, we do not need to fear any storm. In the Lord, we are secure.

Prayer: *Dear Lord, help us not to place our focus on what is temporary, but rather to fix our eyes and hearts firmly on you. Amen*

Thought for the day: No matter what I face, I am made stronger when I focus on God.

Dave Zyronn A. Escalona (Batangas, Philippines)

Giving thanks

Read 1 Corinthians 12:12–26

'Give us this day our daily bread.'
Matthew 6:11 (NRSV)

Eating breakfast one morning, I thought of these words from the Lord's Prayer: 'Give us this day our daily bread.' I suddenly became aware of my gratitude for the many people who were responsible for my cereal and milk, my banana and my cup of coffee. I was humbled as I imagined the many hands labouring to secure my meal.

I thanked God for the provision of food and for all the people who had been involved. In gratitude, I prayed for the farmers who grew and harvested the grains, fruit and coffee and for those who raised and milked the cows. And I prayed for all the people – factory workers, truckers, grocers and many more – whose work made it possible for me to receive these gifts.

We are interdependent, as God created us to be. We are blessed every day by many people we will never know. Being aware of that connection, my food was sweeter that morning, and my heart was full of praise.

Prayer: *Thank you, God, for our daily bread and for the people responsible for bringing it to our tables. Amen*

Thought for the day: Each day I am blessed by many people I will never know.

Sybil Austin Skakle (North Carolina, USA)

I can do all things

Read Philippians 4:10–13

I can do all things through [Christ] who strengthens me.
Philippians 4:13 (NRSV)

In the last week of my dad's life, he didn't complain as he lay in the ICU. Instead, he wanted to be sure that I was getting enough rest at night and that I understood how to handle the affairs of his home. Some days he asked to hear scripture read aloud. He loved Philippians 4:13, 'I can do all things through [Christ] who strengthens me.' He repeated those words with a calm confidence that his good shepherd would lead him along the last stretch of his path on earth.

The apostle Paul had experienced a series of unusual circumstances. He recalled his successes and failures, the times when his cupboard was bare and the times friends provided him home-cooked meals. Yet despite everything he faced, Paul shows us that when we learn to trust in Christ we find contentment.

In whatever we face today God is always at work – both in us and in our circumstances. With God's help, we all will be able to say, 'It really is true! I can do all things through Christ who strengthens me!'

Prayer: *God of strength, open our hearts so that we may learn contentment. Help us always to trust in you and your Son, who strengthens us. Amen*

Thought for the day: No matter my circumstances, I will trust Christ to give me strength.

Peter Caligiuri (Florida, USA)

Lost but found

Read Luke 15:3–7

'If a man owns a hundred sheep, and one of them wanders away, will he not leave the ninety-nine on the hills and go to look for the one that wandered off?'
Matthew 18:12 (NIV)

It was our practice in high school to look for one another's lost items (pens, rulers, pencils, etc.). Whenever a lost item was found, the class prefect would stand in front of the class and shout, 'Lost but found!' The announcement enabled the owners to identify and reclaim their lost items. Motivated by the accolades awarded to finders, everybody was actively involved in the search. Whatever was lost within the school would certainly be found.

In today's scripture reading, Jesus told the parable of the lost sheep, where a shepherd went out to search for one lost sheep. 'I am the good shepherd,' Jesus said (John 10:11). As Christians, we should not lose hope over anyone who leaves the faith. The good shepherd can find any sheep that has wandered off and lost its way. For Jesus said, 'I give them eternal life, and they shall never perish; no one will snatch them out of my hand' (John 10:28). We can trust the good shepherd to bring the lost sheep home. 'Lost but found,' he will announce. And whoever we thought was lost will be lovingly restored to the fold.

Prayer: *Dear God, thank you for caring for each one of us as the shepherd cares for each sheep in the flock. No matter how far we may wander, you always guide us back home. In Jesus' name we pray. Amen*

Thought for the day: When I am lost, Jesus wants to lead me back home.

Olaiya Muyiwa Benralph (Federal Capital Territory, Nigeria)

God's wonderful works

Read Genesis 2:8–17

The Lord God took the man and put him in the Garden of Eden to work it and take care of it.

Genesis 2:15 (NIV)

For much of my working life, I was frequently away from home, many weeks coming home Saturday evening only to be away again on Sunday evening. This meant that after Sunday morning worship at church, I had to attend to a number of domestic chores in the limited time I had left at my disposal. The chore I disliked most was cutting the lawn and tidying up the garden. Often I would have to do this hated work in the rain, otherwise it would be another week before it got done.

Since I have retired, however, a change has come over me. I no longer dislike working in the garden; in fact, it has become my main interest and pastime. I spend a great deal of my days pottering in my beloved garden. We live in an area that is popular with holidaymakers and when I'm working in my front garden, I receive many compliments about my colourful flowers from people new to the area. I thank them and then tell them, 'God and I do it between us. He does the clever part and I do the labouring,' and this sometimes leads to a conversation with them about faith.

Who would have thought that what was once a hated chore could become such a relaxing therapy and, more importantly, a wonderful chance to witness for God with strangers that God puts in my way!

Prayer: *Dear Father, help us to see and to seize the opportunities you give us to witness to your wonderful works. Amen*

Thought for the day: God has placed me in his garden to work it and take care of it.

Tony Coghlan (England, United Kingdom)

'Who are you?'

Read John 1:19–28

John replied in the words of Isaiah the prophet, 'I am the voice of one calling in the wilderness, "Make straight the way for the Lord."'
John 1:23 (NIV)

At church one Sunday I learned of a woman in the community whose husband had just died. They had four children. At God's urging, I attended the funeral to lend my support. I did not talk much. I just sat beside her, listened to her story and helped when needed. After the funeral ceremony was over and all her relatives went home, she asked, 'Who are you? Are you one of my relatives that I have never met? Why did you sit with me until it was over?'

I replied, 'I'm not your relative. I just want to sit with you, listen to your story and offer help to you if you need it.' Then she said, 'Thank you for being with me. My relatives give me a lot of advice, but you don't talk much; you only hear my sad stories. Why?' I said to her, 'Because the God I know is always with me, even the saddest times in my life.'

I have learned from today's scripture reading that when someone asks, 'Who are you?' I should tell that person more about God who saved me than about myself. In such an answer, God becomes greater as I become smaller. For as John the Baptist tells the Jewish priests, I am not the Messiah or a prophet; I am only 'the voice of one calling in the wilderness'. To God be all glory.

Prayer: *Dear God, may we glorify you in our actions and in our words. Make us humble so that we can magnify your name. Amen*

Thought for the day: When I am smaller, God is greater.

Linda Chandra (Banten, Indonesia)

Living signs

Read Matthew 5:14–16

God said, 'Let there be lights in the dome of the sky to separate the day from the night; and let them be for signs and for seasons and for days and years.'
Genesis 1:14 (NRSV)

When I think of signs that keep people safe or offer guidance, I first think of traffic lights, lighthouses and billboards. But we often forget how much more valuable we are as signs that have the potential to show others the hope, joy and direction God can give to them. In a world where there is so much despair and hopelessness, living, practical signs and beacons of hope are important for us all to hold on to.

While God is invisible, God has shown us through Jesus Christ how to make God visible for others. We are to be living signs of God's light of love, drawing people from darkness into the light of life. Sharing a loving word and performing acts of kindness serve as openings to God's kingdom for those who have lost hope. And in this way we make the world a bit brighter.

Prayer: *O Lord, teach us to be beacons of hope, living signs of your transforming power, and active witnesses to your salvation. In the name of Jesus who taught us to pray, 'Our Father in heaven, hallowed be your name, your kingdom come, your will be done, on earth as it is in heaven. Give us today our daily bread. And forgive us our debts, as we also have forgiven our debtors. And lead us not into temptation, but deliver us from the evil one' (Matthew 6:9–13, NIV). Amen*

Thought for the day: My actions and words can lead someone closer to Christ.

Benjamin Ankrah (Ashanti Region, Ghana)

Palm Sunday

Read Colossians 1:7–12

It is God who is at work in you, enabling you both to will and to work for his good pleasure.
Philippians 2:13 (NRSV)

I enjoy needlework. I begin with a blank piece of material, and I start placing the colourful stitches according to the pattern. It doesn't look like much at first, but as I continue to work, a picture emerges. Sometimes I put stitches in the wrong place. Then I have to take them out and try again. I keep going until I have a completed work of art.

When we embark on our journey with Christ, we have no idea what to expect. We are like that blank piece of material waiting for a beautiful picture to take shape. As we continue our journey, the purpose God has for each of us is gradually revealed. We begin to see the work of art we are to become.

Discerning God's will is not always easy. Some of us might get a glimmer of it early in our journey and begin pursuing it. Others of us may need to take a few steps back or rethink our direction before we understand God's plans.

God has a purpose for each of us. We can trust that God's plan will take shape throughout our lives as our relationship with Christ grows. We can all be confident that God is working in us.

Prayer: *Dear God, help us to be hopeful and patient as we seek your plan for us. In Jesus' name. Amen*

Thought for the day: God has a plan for me.

Lorraine Baldus (Michigan, USA)

PRAYER FOCUS: SOMEONE WHO IS STARTING OVER

Choose to rejoice

Read 1 Thessalonians 5:16–24

Though the fig tree doesn't bloom, and there's no produce on the vine; though the olive crop withers, and the fields don't provide food… I will rejoice in the Lord. I will rejoice in the God of my deliverance.
Habakkuk 3:17–18 (CEB)

When I moved to Lucknow, in India, I was longing for a good job and had many interviews. When I couldn't find a job, I became so frustrated that I decided to give up and move back to my hometown. While I was packing my bags, I received a call from a renowned institution informing me of my selection for a position. Then I realised that many times in my life when everything seemed to be falling apart, I simply gave in to my adversities or refused to be led by God. But thankfully, God never left me alone.

Sometimes even when we are praying continuously, we still feel stuck in our problems. It is easy to assume God is not listening and to stop praying and reading our Bible. But that makes us more vulnerable to the chaos of life.

Instead of giving up, we can choose to rejoice, just like Habakkuk. God loves us too much to ever leave us alone. After all, God gave his Son for us. Jesus is the ultimate proof of God's love and faithfulness. God is with us as our trusted companion and will never walk away or let us down.

Prayer: *Thank you, God, for the assurance that you are always with us. Help us to open our hearts to your loving presence. Amen*

Thought for the day: Even when I doubt, God never gives up on me.

Akanksha Singh (Uttar Pradesh, India)

Ears to hear

Read Romans 10:16–21

'Whoever has ears, let them hear.'
Matthew 11:15 (NIV)

Due to a sinus infection, one of my ears became filled with fluid. I could hear clearly out of my good ear, but the other only registered muffled sounds. I became frustrated by my inability to hear sounds I had taken for granted before. I had to ask people to repeat themselves in conversation. Sound distortion threw me off key during praise team rehearsal, and I couldn't hear important details when the team leader gave instructions. For a time, I literally did not have ears to hear.

How often do we suffer from the same affliction in our spiritual lives? Worldly distractions, fear, stubbornness, pride, apathy, selfishness and sin can build up in our hearts and keep us from hearing God's voice. Our pastor preaches a message, but we may catch only part of it because we're distracted. We ask God for guidance, but we might fail to study scripture and miss God's answers. God is always speaking, but sometimes a blockage distorts our hearing.

When my doctor drained the fluid from my ear canal, my full hearing returned. The Great Physician will clear out our spiritual blockages too. We just need to acknowledge our lack of spiritual hearing and turn our hearts towards God.

Prayer: *Father God, please remove the blockages that prevent us from hearing your voice clearly so that we may have ears to hear when you speak. In Jesus' name. Amen*

Thought for the day: When I turn my heart towards God, I can better hear God's voice.

Pat Banta Kreml (Florida, USA)

In your hands

Read Psalm 116:1–7

Trust in the Lord with all your heart and lean not on your own understanding.
Proverbs 3:5 (NIV)

When my wife was diagnosed with an aggressive form of dementia, we were devastated. I watched helplessly as our 27 years of marriage slowly disappeared from her memory. I struggled to make sense of the deep sorrow, frustration and anger I felt. I wanted to know *why*.

I laid my heart bare to God. I prayed honestly, openly and sometimes angrily as I expressed my frustration and my desire for answers. I prayed through tears, pleading with God to heal my beloved wife and to remove my burden of being a full-time caregiver while working a full-time job.

One morning, when it felt like my prayers were going nowhere, I was able to slow down and quiet my mind enough to hear God's message. I needed to pray not for understanding but for faith. I needed to look not for answers but for the courage to trust in God. I began to pray for God's presence in my life and in my heart, and I have grown closer to God than I have ever been.

I know God is working for good (see Romans 8:28). Sometimes I can't see the good, but I know God is faithful and will guide me through this. I don't have the answers, but I have been richly blessed by God's presence, which gives me the strength to cope with the tragedy of my wife's illness.

Prayer: *Loving God, give us the courage to place all things into your hands, to submit our will to yours, with an abundant faith in your promises. Amen*

Thought for the day: I can trust God even when I don't have full understanding.

Michael Albanese (New York, USA)

PRAYER FOCUS: SPOUSES OF PEOPLE WITH DEMENTIA

Maundy Thursday

Read John 13:31–35

'As I have loved you, so you must love one another.'
John 13:34 (NIV)

I remember my first Maundy Thursday worship service. I didn't know what to expect; to be honest, I didn't know what 'Maundy' meant! Maundy, I learned, was a shortened form of the Latin word *mandatum*, which means 'command'. As we see in our verse from John today, Jesus gave his disciples and us a new commandment on that first Maundy Thursday: 'You must love one another.' That night Jesus humbled himself by washing the disciples' feet as he shared a meal with them for the last time before his death. The next day Jesus paid the ultimate price by giving his life for our sins.

The first Maundy Thursday service I attended brought the worshippers to a point of self-reflection. Then the pastor asked for our personal prayer concerns, prayed for us individually, and ended the service with Communion.

When the service was over, I was in tears thinking of the love Christ has for us. His command to us was not just to love someone when it's easy or convenient but to love even when it's hard – like when we are busy or when someone is difficult to love. Some days and some situations are challenging. But we can each pray that we will love one another so that we can show the world what it means to follow Christ.

Prayer: *Father God, thank you for your gift of love. Help us to humble ourselves to love others as Christ has loved us. Amen*

Thought for the day: Loving like Christ begins with humility.

Kathleen Brewer (New Brunswick, Canada)

Good Friday

Read Matthew 26:36–46

*Going a little farther, [Jesus] threw himself on the ground and prayed,
'My Father, if it is possible, let this cup pass from me; yet not what
I want but what you want.'*
Matthew 26:39 (NRSV)

Good Friday reminds me of a time when I found it difficult to do the will
of God. I was serving God in another country, and I felt lonely and wished
I could be back home to be with my people. But then I thought of how
Jesus surrendered himself to God's will even when he did not want to.

As Jesus was about to face crucifixion, he recoiled at the thought of
death. Although he prayed that God would let the cup of death pass from
him, he also asked that God's will be done. Jesus knew that, although
God's will looked bitter at the time, the end result would be good.

Thinking of Jesus' readiness to follow God's will, I was encouraged to
continue serving where I was as long as God wanted me there. I knew
that in the end, good would come from it.

We won't always feel like sacrificing ourselves – our time or our efforts –
to do the things God wants us to do. But on this Good Friday, let us respond
as Jesus did, saying, 'Not what I want but what you want.'

Prayer: *Dear God, help us to do your will in all situations. Give us
strength to persevere when we feel discouraged. In Jesus' name.
Amen*

Thought for the day: Even when it is difficult, I will do what God has
called me to do.

Enid Adah Nyinomujuni (Dar es Salaam, Tanzania)

Trust in God

Read Matthew 27:38–46

'He trusts in God. Let God rescue him now.'
Matthew 27:43 (NIV)

For years, I prayed for a baby. I longed to look into the eyes of my newborn and hear the little sounds that a newborn makes. Through all the waiting, fertility screenings and treatments, I prayed and waited.

During my years of waiting, I was hesitant to declare my trust in God, especially to those who weren't believers. I was afraid that they would think, *If her God is so trustworthy, why haven't her prayers been answered?*

As we read in today's quoted verse, Jesus was mocked for his faith as he hung on the cross. To onlookers, it appeared that God had abandoned Jesus, and Jesus even poured his heart out to God asking why he had been forsaken. God didn't rescue Jesus from the cross as his followers had hoped because God had a much bigger plan that would make redemption possible.

We often cannot see God's plan. We think, *If only God would intervene and fix my problem*. But if we continue to trust in God, we are in good company. Even if others mock our trust, God is trustworthy. We have every reason to declare boldly our trust in God.

Prayer: *Dear God, help us to trust you when our prayers seem unanswered. Give us courage to declare our trust in you. Amen*

Thought for the day: God is always worthy of my trust.

Susan Kerrigan (Washington, USA)

Easter Sunday

Read John 20:1–9

Early on the first day of the week, while it was still dark, Mary Magdalene went to the tomb and saw that the stone had been removed from the entrance.
John 20:1 (NIV)

One Easter Sunday, my pastor preached on the account of the resurrection in John 20. I don't recall what the main point of her message was, because the phrase 'while it was still dark' captured my attention.

My wife and I had been going through a difficult time regarding destructive choices that our teenage son was making. We had lost control, and we knew it. Our situation seemed hopeless, and it felt like it would go on forever.

But though the scripture reading began with 'while it was still dark,' as it continued it became clear that God had already been at work! Not only had the stone been rolled away but our Lord Jesus Christ had risen! In a time of perpetual sadness and despair, the Holy Spirit whispered to my heart that, although my outward circumstances had not changed, the God of resurrection was at work in our son's life. Hope and faith were kindled in my wife and me that Easter morning. How wonderful that our loving God speaks to us at our lowest moments, giving us the hope of resurrection and new life to come!

Prayer: *Dear Father, thank you for the stories of hope we find in scripture, especially that of your Son's resurrection. Help us to trust in that living hope. Amen*

Thought for the day: Even when we don't perceive it, our loving God is at work.

Jeff Evans (Texas, USA)

Valuable to God

Read Matthew 13:44–46

'The kingdom of heaven is like treasure hidden in a field. When a man found it, he hid it again, and then in his joy went and sold all he had and bought that field.'

Matthew 13:44 (NIV)

I used to think that I was not valuable to God. I would think to myself, *I am not as good looking as that person. I do not have any important skills. I'm not good enough.* Sometimes these thoughts started with something as simple as not being invited to an event and feeling rejected. Other times, I found myself brooding over painful words said to me or things done to me.

Meditating on today's verse from Matthew helped me to see how the king of kings and God of the universe feels about me. In God's eyes I am a treasure who brings delight and joy. God believes we are worth giving up everything. So as I think about Christ being born and dying on the cross, I now understand that sacrifice in light of this parable.

We understand how much something is worth by the price that has been paid. Jesus gave it all for me on the cross. Therefore I can no longer go on living another day feeling like I do not count. I am learning to look at myself and say out loud, 'I am valuable!'

Prayer: *Father, thank you for loving me and embracing me. Thank you for giving your all for me. Amen*

Thought for the day: I am special to God.

Selina Machado (Blantyre, Malawi)

Forgiveness is essential

Read Psalm 130

If you, Lord, kept a record of sins, Lord, who could stand? But with you there is forgiveness, so that we can, with reverence, serve you.
Psalm 130:3–4 (NIV)

I recently left a company I had been instrumental in building over the past decade. I was in a leadership role, so the choice to leave was difficult. I could not explain exactly what was wrong, but I knew things were changing. When I shared my concerns about where the company was headed, colleagues I once trusted turned their backs on me. I walked away, feeling broken and defeated.

The traditional stages of grief include denial, anger and depression, followed by eventual acceptance. In Psalm 130, God makes it clear that forgiveness is also essential. Although time eased the pain of loss and betrayal, without the extra step of forgiveness I was consumed by a desire for retribution. Wanting bad things to happen to the people who hurt me was not healthy, and it kept me focused on their failings instead of acknowledging my own. As I stewed over the injustice of my situation, I was unable to see that God could use this painful experience to strengthen my faith.

We cannot move forward with God if our energy is spent nursing old wounds or hoping for another's misfortune. Instead, we can seek God's wisdom and comfort as we work through the pain, remaining open to what God has in store for us.

Prayer: *Dear heavenly Father, help us to forgive so that we can let go of the past and grow closer to you. Amen*

Thought for the day: By forgiving those who hurt me, I can better serve God.

Reese Delaney (Georgia, USA)

Enough

Read 1 Kings 17:8–16

The jar of meal was not emptied, neither did the jug of oil fail.
1 Kings 17:16 (NRSV)

Our family often welcomes foster children into our home. Earlier this year, our case worker asked if we could host a five-year-old boy. He had cerebral palsy, a seizure disorder and spoke a different language than our family. We have five other children, and life already felt busy. I told the case worker we would let her know soon – fully expecting to say no.

My Bible reading that day was the story of the widow of Zarephath. Because of a drought, she had only a handful of flour and a little bit of oil left when Elijah asked her for bread. It was difficult, but she gave him all she had. Then, God gave her a miracle – day after day, she used the flour and oil, and the supply did not run out.

As I read about the widow, I felt the Holy Spirit's nudge to say yes to the placement request. It would be easier to say no; but if I did, I knew I would miss this chance to experience God's provision.

We took this young boy into our home. At times it was difficult, but like the widow's flour and oil, our time and love did not run out. As with the widow of Zarephath, God provided all we needed. When God calls us, it is a blessing to say yes.

Prayer: *Generous God, help us to trust that you will provide all we need as we serve others. Amen*

Thought for the day: It is a blessing to say yes to God's call.

Kate Rietema (Michigan, USA)

Light load

Read Matthew 11:28–30

'Come to me, all you that are weary and are carrying heavy burdens, and I will give you rest.'

Matthew 11:28 (NRSV)

My life seemed fine as I grew from a child into an adult. When I went to school to get my bachelor's degree, everything went well. Even though I wasn't the smartest in class, I finished my education. After that, I began working at a company. I have been fortunate to earn enough income to fulfil my needs.

Then one day a doctor said that I had cancer. My world turned upside down. I cried. I never expected to receive this news. Because of the cancer, I now tire quickly and will have to take medicine for the rest of my life.

Every day I go to chapel. After my diagnosis, I began praying and asking, 'Lord, why do I have to go through this? Can I afford it?' One day, I felt as if God were taking my hand and whispering, 'Come to me, all you that are weary and are carrying heavy burdens, and I will give you rest.' I opened my Bible and looked for the verse. I read it over and over again until I finally felt calm. With this verse to accompany me, I slowly started to enjoy my days. I know that God is always with me. I don't know how long I will live, but my burden feels light.

Prayer: *O God, help us to remember that you are always present for us. Thank you for sharing our burdens so that they become light. Amen*

Thought for the day: I don't know what my future holds, but I know God is with me.

Waspati Ken Wardani (Jarkarta, Indonesia)

God's plans for me

Read Ephesians 2:1–10

We are God's handiwork, created in Christ Jesus to do good works, which God prepared in advance for us to do.
Ephesians 2:10 (NIV)

I had a plan for the next few hours: take a walk with my husband, eat lunch and attend an online Bible study. The timing would be tight, but I would be able to do it all.

When my husband and I started our walk, I spotted our neighbour. I felt led to talk to her, and I got to know her on a deeper level. Then near the end of our walk, we stopped to talk with another neighbour. She told us she was experiencing a major struggle, and we promised to pray for her.

Only 30 minutes before Bible study, my sister called with exciting news. I had not yet eaten lunch and feared I would be late. But then I saw an email from the study leader asking me to offer the opening prayer, so I quickly ate my lunch and joined the meeting on time.

In the past, a day like this would have stressed me out. But since studying Ephesians 2:10 with my Bible study group, I have begun praying that God will open my eyes and heart to God's plans for me. God often calls me to listen, share and do good works. I strive to be willing and joyful as I fulfil God's purpose for me.

Prayer: *Heavenly Father, grant us the wisdom, grace and courage to accomplish the works you call us to do. In Jesus' name we pray. Amen*

Thought for the day: I will open my heart so that I can discover what God has in store for me.

Terry J. Burns (Florida, USA)

Everlasting love

Read Matthew 9:9–13

'I have loved you with an everlasting love.'
Jeremiah 31:3 (NIV)

Binky was our Yorkshire terrier. He wasn't the typical tiny, silky, yapping creature you might imagine. He had been the largest of his litter. His tail had not been docked; his ears flopped. Despite his pedigree, according to breed standards he was a failure. To us, however, he was a real character: barking at the mail carrier with a big dog bark, chasing cats from the garden and always ready for another walk. And sometimes he would glare and show his teeth at us. Nevertheless, he was part of the family, and we loved him.

We all need to love and be loved. But even if we have been Christians for years, we can struggle to believe that God really loves us. In our gospel passage today, Jesus shows the nature of God's everlasting love when he seeks out those who have been rejected by society. Jesus spends quality time with them and calls them to follow him.

When we allow Jesus to lead us to God, God accepts us, however imperfect or 'different' we may be. God patiently heals our deepest hurts and hang-ups because we are all part of God's beloved family.

Prayer: *Dear God, we come to you today with all our hurts and failures. Help us to know that you accept us and love us always. Amen*

Thought for the day: God doesn't see me as imperfect, just one of the family.

April McIntyre (England, United Kingdom)

Road to Emmaus

Read Luke 24:13–35

When he was at the table with them, he took bread, gave thanks, broke it and began to give it to them. Then their eyes were opened and they recognised him, and he disappeared from their sight.
Luke 24:30–31 (NIV)

Over 55 years ago a friend gave my wife and me a picture that portrays Jesus walking with the disciples on the road to Emmaus. No matter where we live, this picture hangs in a prominent place, and I see it every day. One day I saw it in a new way and realised that parts of my own spiritual journey are much like the disciples' experience on the road to Emmaus.

The disciples had learned to trust and rely on Jesus as they listened to his teaching, committed themselves to follow him and witnessed his miraculous power to transform lives. With Jesus' death, that trust was broken, replaced by doubt and fear. But Jesus joined them on the road, encouraged them through the words of scripture and performed an act he knew would cause them to recognise him – demonstrating that he would always be with them.

When I have experienced confusion and despair, Jesus has revealed himself to me and assured me of his continual presence. Just as Jesus was with those early disciples on their walk to Emmaus, he comes and meets us along our way and helps us understand the meaning of God's word within our own circumstances, assuring us that we are never alone.

Prayer: *Eternal God, we give thanks that no matter what happens, we can rely on your presence to guide and strengthen us. Restore our hope as we continue on this journey. In Jesus' name. Amen*

Thought for the day: Jesus is with me even when I am not aware of it.

Robert M. Terhune (Oregon, USA)

PRAYER FOCUS: THOSE UNAWARE OF JESUS' PRESENCE

Making a difference

Read Ephesians 4:11–16

You are the body of Christ, and each one of you is a part of it.
1 Corinthians 12:27 (NIV)

The year 2020 may have come to an end, but it will not be easily forgotten. It was a year that brought horrific pain, loss and change in the lives of many.

But the pandemic also brought positive change. Working from home helped some people realise that they have missed spending time with family and friends. Many who used to spend hours working late have started to appreciate a better balance between work and home life. The pandemic has also highlighted the importance of mental health, so often neglected in a highly competitive society.

Seeing so many people suffering from the effects of the pandemic, I have strongly felt the call to join mental health volunteers to help others overcome their adversity. Sometimes, a listening ear or an encouraging word can make a positive difference in someone's life. In Ephesians 4:11–16, God calls on different people to come together to provide works of service so that the body of Christ may be built up, as each part does its work in love.

God can turn ashes into beauty through people from all walks of life banding together in love to make a difference in the lives of others.

Prayer: *Heavenly Father, thank you for the different talents you have given to each of us and for opportunities to use them to make a difference. Amen*

Thought for the day: God can turn ashes to beauty through my willingness to care for others.

Agnes Wee (Singapore)

Great plans

Read 1 Kings 19:1–15

Elijah was a human being like us.
James 5:17 (NRSV)

Years ago, I ran a large community outreach event for our church. Thousands of people came, and it went well. But at the end, one person made a critical remark, and I went home thinking only about what they had said. Because of that one complaint, I felt like the entire event had failed.

In 1 Kings 19, we read how Elijah experienced something similar. He had recently performed two of his greatest miracles: defeating the prophets of Baal and ending the drought with his prayer. Elijah was doing great things with God: helping vulnerable people, destroying false gods and saving a region from disaster. But then Jezebel threatened him. After all his great work, Elijah lost his confidence, went off by himself and wanted to die. That one negative experience outweighed everything else.

Elijah's loss of confidence is all too familiar. After all, James 5:17 tells us that Elijah was just like us. But when God brought Elijah food for strength and gave him a task, he realised that God still had good plans for him. And he accomplished more great things through God's power and grace. Just as God still had great plans for Elijah, God also has great plans for us.

Prayer: *Dear God, show us opportunities to grow through criticism and accomplish even more for you. Amen*

Thought for the day: I can turn criticism into an opportunity to seek God's guidance and grace.

Bob LaForge (New Jersey, USA)

PRAYER FOCUS: SOMEONE I HAVE HURT WITH MY CRITICISM   117

Safe place

Read Psalm 36:5–9

God is our refuge and strength, an ever-present help in trouble.
Psalm 46:1 (NIV)

My daughter works at an alternative school for students with needs that cannot be met in a traditional public school setting. Since my retirement, I have occasionally worked as a substitute teacher at the school. In each room there is a designated 'safe place' where students can go for a break when they are feeling overwhelmed or fearful about a situation. The safe place is located in a quiet part of the room, and the creative use of materials and furniture enhances the illusion of isolation by providing a barrier between the occupants of the space and other students in the room.

We all need a safe place sometimes. I believe that Christians have access to this safe place through Christ: 'In Christ we have bold and confident access to God through faith in him' (Ephesians 3:12, CEB). Today's scripture reading reassures me when I am scared or overwhelmed. I know that in the quietness of my heart, I can take refuge under God's wings where I find comfort, peace and joy.

The Bible tells us many times that God desires to be 'our refuge and strength'. In the safe place God provides, we can find courage and hope.

Prayer: *Dear God, thank you for your presence and for your desire to protect us. Help us trust that you will never fail or forsake us. Amen*

Thought for the day: When I am afraid, I can take refuge in Christ.

Cathy Fooshee (Kansas, USA)

Growing in gratitude

Read Ephesians 3:14–19

Be rooted and built up in [Christ Jesus], be established in faith, and overflow with thanksgiving just as you were taught.
Colossians 2:7 (CEB)

In the book of Colossians, Paul poured out his heart as he urged Christians to build their lives on Jesus. 'Be rooted and built up in him,' Paul wrote. Any tree that is firm and solid has roots extended down into the ground, and its deep roots prevent the tree from being knocked over. As believers, we are like these trees. We can root ourselves in the truth of God's word, which keeps us from being moved or shaken – no matter how turbulent the circumstance. Rooted in Christ, our faith can withstand thoughts and emotions that try to stir up turmoil inside us. As a result, our hearts will begin to overflow with gratitude.

A thankful heart is victorious. It resists fear and creates a contagious atmosphere of joyful hope and peace around us. So, the next time negativity tries to rush in and pour out of our mouths, we can stop it with a word of thankfulness. Gratitude can neutralise toxic thoughts, fill our hearts and minds with the powerful force of faith, and positively affect everyone around us.

Prayer: *Dear God, help us to stay rooted in your love, grounded in your word and ever growing in gratitude and grace. Amen*

Thought for the day: When I am rooted in God's word, my faith grows strong.

Nelson Nwosu (Anambra, Nigeria)

Hands

Read Matthew 8:1–4

'Look at my hands and my feet. It is I myself! Touch me and see'…
When he had said this, he showed them his hands and feet.
Luke 24:39–40 (NIV)

Looking at my heavily veined and arthritic hands, I am reminded of an evocative photograph of the hands of four generations of family members, baby to great-grandmother, illustrating the changes that a lifetime brings.

So it was with Jesus' hands. His baby hands: tiny, helpless, dependent. In childhood: playing, learning and exploring, responding to his mother's love and training. His adult hands: strong and toughened through working as a carpenter, yet gently blessing children, healing the sick and the blind, and even restoring life. How often those hands were lifted in compassionate prayer to his heavenly Father: for his friends and enemies; for his Father's will to be done and for his own needs as he endured rejection and suffering to fulfil the purpose for which God had sent him.

Those hands, which had only been used for good and in loving service, so brutally torn, broken and bleeding by the nails fixing him to the cross, speak of his sacrifice to free us from sin's punishment. Even with nailed hands, Jesus ensured a secure home for his mother with John, promised mercy for the penitent thief and prayed for forgiveness for those crucifying Him.

When he was risen, Jesus' scarred hands proved to those disciples who were slow to believe that he really was alive, and they prepared breakfast on the shore for some of them. Finally, Jesus' hands were raised to bless his disciples before his ascension.

Prayer: *Dear Lord, please equip our hands for your service. Amen*

Thought for the day: How may the Lord use my hands today?

Hazel V. Thompson (England, United Kingdom)

Pick up and pray

Read Romans 12:1–8

Devote yourselves to prayer, being watchful and thankful.
Colossians 4:2 (NIV)

My husband and I like to go on daily walks along the roadways of our rural town. Several years ago, we decided to pick up litter in the ditches along the streets where we walk. It is rewarding both to get exercise and fresh air and to help beautify God's earth. But it can be frustrating also. We find that after cleaning up an area, more litter accumulates within a few days. At one point, I became angry at the repeat offenders, but then I changed my way of thinking and started praying. With every piece of litter I pick up, I pray for the person who threw it there. Almost immediately God changed my anger and frustration into forgiveness and empathy.

We can reshape our thoughts and attitudes with prayer. Prayer can turn hate into love, fear into trust, anger into forgiveness and despair into joy. As we remind ourselves to pray when confronted by negative thoughts, such as fear and anger, we can reshape our thoughts to conform to the thoughts and ways of Jesus. God's gift of prayer has awesome power!

Prayer: *Dear God, thank you for giving us the privilege of prayer. As we pray, reshape our minds to conform to your will. Amen*

Thought for the day: Prayer can change my mind and my life.

Jan Towne (Virginia, USA)

A close relationship

Read Luke 10:38–42

'Mary has chosen the better part, which will not be taken away from her.'
Luke 10:42 (NRSV)

Almost every Saturday and Sunday I am busy serving at my church, which is one of the ways I respond to God's call and give thanks for Jesus' sacrifice on the cross. However, I am often worn out on the weekends, because I also have a job that requires a long daily commute during the week.

When we get tired physically, our enthusiasm to worship may decrease. However, in today's quoted scripture we are reminded that the best part of worship – sitting at the feet of God – can never be taken away from us. Sitting at God's feet involves not only prayer but also building a close personal relationship with God by reading scripture and listening to sermons.

When I started to strengthen my relationship with God, my service in church began to feel different to me. I became more excited about worship and had a renewed desire to give my best every time. Christianity is more than just a religion; it is a relationship between our heavenly Father and us, God's children.

Prayer: *Dear God, draw us into a closer relationship with you so that we may know you better each day. Help us to find renewed commitment in our service to you. Amen*

Thought for the day: Spending time with God renews me to better serve God and others.

Renaldo Yosua (West Java, Indonesia)

Weathering life's storms

Read Psalm 107:28–30

Then they cried out to the Lord in their trouble, and he brought them out of their distress.

Psalm 107:28 (NIV)

When a sudden squall sent me scurrying for cover, I shared my shelter with a stranger. I listened intently as he listed a litany of troubles he was currently experiencing, and I wondered how one person could carry so many burdens. 'I get a little help from the Lord,' he told me with a twinkle in his eye.

When the storm abated and the man left, the Lord was still uppermost in my mind. I thought about the way Jesus rebuked the waves on the sea of Galilee, and how the storm became calm. But Jesus then chastised the disciples for their lack of faith, because they had panicked.

The psalmist says, 'They cried out to the Lord in their trouble, and he brought them out of their distress' (Psalm 107:28). How well God knows us! How gently he corrects us when we get things wrong. When my troubles seem insurmountable, I call for his help more often than I can say. I recognise his hand on my life, and I'm content.

Prayer: *Dear Lord, help us to trust in you at all times, especially when we are hit by life's storms. Amen*

Thought for the day: The Lord is my refuge in times of trouble (see Psalm 9:9).

Pauline Pullan (England, United Kingdom)

A crucial ingredient

Read Matthew 5:13–16

'You are the salt of the earth.'
Matthew 5:13 (CEB)

One of my favourite meals is pinto beans cooked with diced onion, sweet pepper, tomato, garlic and salt. Although we cannot see salt in our food, it is crucial. We always know whether or not it is present – too much can make a dish inedible, and too little leaves it tasting bland. Just the right amount ensures a tasty meal.

Salt is important in our faith as well. Jesus tells us to be salt of the earth. I think this means we should show Jesus' love to the world in such a way that we bring forth its full flavour. Part of our Christian responsibility is not only to make ourselves pleasing to God but also to relate to others in a way that helps them become pleasing to God. What a big challenge Jesus has set before us!

Being salt to the world is both humbling and empowering. We are humbled because being salt requires us to direct our attention towards others. And we are empowered because we trust the Spirit and share Jesus' ministry as we strive to make the world pleasing to God.

Prayer: *O Lord, guide us to be salt in the world as we show your love to others. We pray as Jesus taught us, 'Father, hallowed be your name, your kingdom come. Give us each day our daily bread. Forgive us our sins, for we also forgive everyone who sins against us. And lead us not into temptation' (Luke 11:2–4, NIV). Amen*

Thought for the day: I please God when I relate to others with love.

William G. Heck (North Carolina, USA)

God who weeps with us

Read John 11:32–36

[God's] anger lasts only a moment, but his favour lasts a lifetime; weeping may stay for the night, but rejoicing comes in the morning.
Psalm 30:5 (NIV)

My son, who was 19 and a first-year medical student, died suddenly in a swimming accident. We were devastated. In our pain we questioned God: *Why did this happen when his future seemed so bright?* Many friends visited us to comfort and pray with us. One of my husband's friends wrote a letter, in which he said, 'You must be wondering where God was at that time. He was right there weeping with you.' These words comforted me, and I was reminded of the time Jesus grieved with Martha and Mary when their brother Lazarus died (see John 11:35). God is indeed right by our side grieving when we grieve.

As time went by, I decided to enrol in seminary to study the scriptures and learn more about the God who weeps with us. I was ordained and worked as a pastor for a few years. I was able to empathise with families who were going through an experience of loss and grief.

Four decades after the loss of my son, God is still strengthening me. I have known God's grace and comfort through the love and encouragement of my husband, my children and my church community. Our God of compassion and love is good all the time, and I know that a day will come when I will join my son in God's heavenly presence.

Prayer: *Loving Father, thank you for your steadfast love and abiding presence. Fill us with your grace and peace, especially in times of pain and brokenness. Amen*

Thought for the day: When I weep, God weeps with me.

Navamani Peter (Karnataka, India)

Perspective

Read Matthew 6:25–34

'Look at the birds of the air; they do not sow or reap or store away in barns, and yet your heavenly Father feeds them. Are you not much more valuable than they?'

Matthew 6:26 (NIV)

Between being a full-time student, training for a sports season, flying airplanes and all of the studying that goes along with those tasks, my daily schedule often drains my energy and leaves me feeling overwhelmed. I often lose track of time and forget to make space in my day for God.

My situation is not unique. All across the world, people must complete tasks in order to fulfil expectations, personal goals or work. It can be easy to become overly focused on our current situation and lose sight of the big picture. However, God has a purpose for us all, and a God that great deserves our attention.

When we make God a priority in our lives, live according to God's guidance and switch our focus to what God has planned for us rather than our daily tasks, our burdens become lighter and we can find comfort and rest in the promises of God. Since God provides for even the smallest of animals, we can have faith that God will provide for us.

Prayer: *Dear God, give us strength and help us to focus on your will rather than our own. Thank you for the blessings you have given us. Help us to use them to carry out your will. Amen*

Thought for the day: I will not lose hope, for God will provide.

Trevor Turco (Texas, USA)

In the background

Read Romans 16:21–27

Whatever you do, work at it with all your heart, as working for the Lord.
Colossians 3:23 (NIV)

Through several generations, various members of my family have been involved in ministry. One was a pastor, another was a missionary, two others were on the staff of different ministries, and several have served as volunteers. Although I have volunteered through the years, my main ministry now is as a Christian writer. I spend long hours researching, reading and writing. Since my work takes place where others can't see it happening, some people assume that I am not heavily involved in church work.

In his letters, the apostle Paul mentioned various people who had done good work where others could not see it. In today's reading, Paul lists the names of several of them. While Phoebe tops that list in Romans 16:1, I am partial to the one who identified himself in Romans 16:22: 'I, Tertius, who wrote down this letter, greet you in the Lord.' Like me, Tertius was performing his ministry in the background.

While we may take for granted the work of those like Tertius, it's important to remember that not all work in ministry is visible to us. Nevertheless, that work is vital to the spreading of the gospel.

Prayer: *Gracious Lord, thank you for those who spread the gospel in ways that are not always visible. Give them the assurance that their work is important and needed. In the name of Jesus. Amen*

Thought for the day: Regardless of my task, God knows the work I do.

Mary Hunt Webb (New Mexico, USA)

Always there

Read Isaiah 43:1–7

The Lord says… 'Do not fear, for I have redeemed you; I have summoned you by name; you are mine.'
Isaiah 43:1 (NIV)

One of my aunts routinely mailed copies of *El Aposento Alto* – the Spanish language edition of *The Upper Room* – to her nieces, nephews and friends. Through the daily devotional, I learnt about Jesus and loving God. I kept every copy she sent.

At age 15, I declared my independence from my parents because they did not believe in me. I stopped studying the arts so I could pursue a career where I could support myself. Around this time, I also started attending church. But eventually, while trying to achieve my goals, I left the church and began to live a life of excess.

After seven years, I completed my doctorate, but I still wasn't happy. I began to experience an existential crisis, so once again I read my old copies of *El Aposento Alto*. The stories were as relevant as when they were first published. During this time I realised that God has always been there for me.

I have since returned to my faith community, and my joy is complete. God dwells in my heart and guides my life and faith. I remain grateful that despite my failings, God stood by me. God's love was manifested through my family, my church and the stories in the daily devotional.

Prayer: *Faithful God, thank you for remaining faithful to us even when we turn from you. Fill us with your wisdom and give us the courage to trust in your saving grace. Amen*

Thought for the day: God will always accompany me on my journey.

Carlos D. Ortiz (Puerto Rico)

A reconciling dinner

Read Matthew 5:43–48

'Love your enemies and pray for those who persecute you.'
Matthew 5:44 (NRSV)

The young couple who lived below my flat frequently played loud music at night. Sometimes I would ask them politely to turn down their music.

One Saturday, the music was particularly loud. Frustrated, once again I asked my neighbours to turn their music down. The young man refused. 'I think you're obsessing over it,' he responded. Having gotten nowhere, I returned to bed. But I regretted that the conversation hadn't gone well. I wanted to make peace, so I offered the only thing I could think of – dinner.

When the day of our dinner arrived, the young man, Brody, arrived alone, since his girlfriend had to work. It felt awkward, but I pressed on, wanting him to know I held no grudges. After our meal, my relationship with the couple improved. Once, when my car wouldn't start, Brody helped me get to an appointment on time.

To live out our identity as God's children, we are called to love even those who don't love us. Extending kindness towards my neighbours required a willingness to respond with love. God has placed people in our lives who may challenge our ability to love them. How do we respond?

Prayer: *Dear Lord, loving people who are challenging to us requires more than human strength. Grant us your power to love them as you love us. Amen*

Thought for the day: With Christ's strength, I can always respond with love.

Allison Wilson Lee (Florida, USA)

Small group questions

Wednesday 4 January

1 Recall a time when you were looking for meaning in life. Where did you find it? How did your relationship with Christ develop during that time?

2 In what ways did the early years of your Christian life set the tone for how you would live out your Christian faith? How has the way you live your faith changed over time?

3 Who taught you how to be a believer in Christ? How did they teach you? In what ways did they shape the faith you have today?

4 Do you find it easier to tell others about your faith or show it by the way you live your life? Why? What spiritual practices help you to share your faith in both words and actions?

5 Think of someone in your life with whom you can share your faith. How will you show that person what it means to be a Christian? How can you encourage them to live a life of faith?

Wednesday 11 January

1 When have you felt lost and out of place? Who or what helped you overcome those feelings?

2 Has anyone ever told you that they've noticed your faith in Christ? If so, what did they notice? When have you noticed someone else's faith? How did their faith strengthen yours?

3 When have you prayed for something and received a different answer than what you expected from God? Was the answer what you truly needed, or did it leave you feeling unsatisfied? How do you respond to unexpected answers to prayer?

4 Why do you think we tend to seek contentment in our surroundings? What prayers and scripture passages remind you of the joy that can only be found in Christ?

5 How are you encouraged by the idea that what you do in God's name can bring God glory? What daily practices help you focus on God and glorify God through your actions?

Wednesday 18 January

1 Where do you feel closest to God and best able to clear your mind? Why do you think that location helps you connect with God? Describe how it feels to be in a sacred place.

2 Why do you think solitude can help people feel closer to God? Do you find it easier to connect with God when you're alone or with others? Why?

3 Have you ever heard an audible voice from God? If so, describe the experience. If not, in what ways do you notice God communicating with you?

4 Describe a time when you realised that God was answering your prayers but not in the way you were expecting. How did you respond?

5 How do you make time to talk with God and to listen for God's answers? What helps you pause and remain quiet so that you can hear God's response?

Wednesday 25 January

1 Why do you think communicating with someone virtually is so different from being with them in person? In what ways do you intentionally strengthen your connections with others, both in person and virtually?

2 What character traits do you think others see in you? What do you hope they can see in you? In what ways do you strive to represent Christ?

3 When have you felt God's encouragement? How did you experience it? How does reading scripture and observing creation help

you feel more connected to God when it seems like God is not responding to you?

4 How do you show those around you that you love them? When do you most clearly feel the love of those around you? When do you feel God's love most strongly? How do you show your love for God?

5 Why do you think it brings God joy when we acknowledge God's love for us? How does God's love encourage you to deepen your relationship with God?

Wednesday 1 February

1 Describe a time when you had high hopes that did not come to fruition. How did you feel? Did that situation change your relationship with God?

2 Have you ever felt that God was punishing you when your life was not going well? Why or why not? What scripture passages help you trust that God is present in your situation and working for good?

3 Today's writer spent seven months feeling distant from God. Have you ever been distant from God? Why? What brought you back to God? What did you learn from that experience?

4 When your situation does not resolve in the way you had hoped, how do you respond? Is your faith strengthened or shaken in such times? How does returning to God's presence bring you peace?

5 Name your favourite Bible story in which someone reunites with God. Why do you like this story? In what ways does it remind you of how important it is to return to God, no matter how distant you might feel?

Wednesday 8 February

1 Do you struggle with comparing yourself to others or finding your identity in your accomplishments? Why do you think it is easy to want to compare ourselves to others? How do you remain focused on what truly matters?

2 What does scripture say about how God sees you? When you remind yourself of what God thinks of you, do you find it easier to stop worrying about what others think? Why or why not?

3 In what ways does your faith community remind you that you are a child of God? How does remembering that you are God's child keep you focused on what is eternally significant?

4 In what ways do you invest in your relationship with Christ? When you are actively working on strengthening that relationship, what changes do you notice in yourself and the way you view others?

5 How might you encourage the people in your life who seem to be struggling with low self-esteem? Name specific ways you can remind them of their identity in Christ.

Wednesday 15 February

1 What task seems never-ending for you? In what ways do you try to work around it or try to make it easier next time?

2 When you are faced with challenges and stress, do you want to get it all over with at once? Why or why not? How do you feel when you have to wait for problems to resolve?

3 How does the fact that new worries come each day encourage you to rely more heavily on God? What scripture passages bring you peace as you face each new struggle?

4 In what ways have you found joy in the spiritual practice of discernment? What spiritual practices best help you remain joyful and at peace amid life's challenges?

5 How do you remind yourself to depend on God each day? In what ways do you lean on your faith community in difficult times? Where else do you find support and comfort?

Wednesday 22 February

1 When you have not seen someone in a long time, how do you get in touch with them? In what ways do you and your loved ones encourage one another in your faith walks, even from a distance?

2 What scripture passages remind you that God's hand is always open to you? How does reading scripture regularly call you back to God's presence?

3 When you feel overwhelmed by the chaos and uncertainty in the world, what brings you peace? Where and when do you most strongly feel God's presence?

4 Who in your life encourages you to reach out and remain near to God? How do you encourage those around you to do the same?

5 What does it mean to you that God is always ready to take your hand and offer you new life? What does new life in God look like?

Wednesday 1 March

1 Describe your favourite prayer practice. What makes this practice meaningful and sustainable for you? What does this practice teach you about God and prayer?

2 Do you find that devotionals like *The Upper Room*, books or other resources enrich your faith and prayers? If so, how? If not, where do you find the most enrichment?

3 If you track your prayers and petitions, what have you observed about your prayers by doing so? If you don't, how do you remain aware of the ways your prayers are being answered?

4 Do you tend to offer more petition prayers or thanksgiving prayers? Is it good to bring our petitions to God as well as our thanks? Explain.

5 When have you had a petition turn into a blessing or thanksgiving? What did you learn about God, yourself and others through that experience?

Wednesday 8 March

1 Did you recognise the names Jochebed, Shiphrah and Puah? Why do you think many people are unfamiliar with these names and so many other biblical women?

2 Why do you think it is important to remember the names of people in the Bible? When was the last time you came across a name in scripture that you did not recognise?

3 Name an often-forgotten biblical woman who stands out in your mind. Why does she stand out for you? What does this woman or her life teach you?

4 Why do you think it is easy to overlook the people we do not know personally who make our daily life easier? What spiritual practices and prayers help you to keep those people and their work in the front of your mind?

5 What women have had the biggest impact on your life? Why? How will you honour them or show them your appreciation for all that they have done for you?

Wednesday 15 March

1 Does your church have an outreach programme like the writer's church? If so, describe the programme. If not, describe any similar programmes you participate in or have heard about.

2 In what ways do you offer your time, resources and support to people in need? How have you observed your efforts making a difference for the people you serve?

3 How does your behaviour and mindset change during Lent? How do you treat others differently in this season? Why?

4 What does it mean for you to see the face of Jesus in the people you meet? Does seeing Jesus in others change the way you interact with them? How do you keep your heart and mind open to the needs of others?

5 Name several needs you have observed in your community. How will you seek to fulfil those needs? How will you encourage your faith community to join your efforts?

Wednesday 22 March

1 Describe a spiritual or life lesson you have learned by spending time in nature. Why do you think we can learn so much by observing nature?

2 Do you ever feel like you need to be resilient and unbreakable? What scripture passages remind you that we don't always need to remain unbreakable?

3 When has brokenness in your life led you to new, beautiful growth? How did that experience affect your faith journey?

4 What does it mean to embody both resilience and brokenness at the same time? In what ways do your life and faith change depending on whether you are feeling resilient, broken or both?

5 Who in scripture most embodied resilience and brokenness? Did they embody just one at a time? Both at once? How does their story encourage and inspire you?

Wednesday 29 March

1 What is your first response when you lose something? What helps you find the lost item? How does it feel to find something that has been lost?

2 The students in today's meditation were motivated to search for lost items because they would receive accolades from their peers. What motivates you to help others? Why?

3 What do you find the most comforting and meaningful about the parable of the lost sheep? How has this parable influenced your life and your faith over time?

4   If you have ever wandered away from God, how did the good shepherd find you and lovingly bring you back? How can it be encouraging to someone who has wandered away to know that the good shepherd is always nearby?

5   When someone you care about leaves the faith, how do you respond? How do you remain hopeful for their return? What helps you to find peace in the situation?

Wednesday 5 April

1   Have you ever watched a loved one struggle with memory loss or another health condition? What was that like? How did that experience affect your relationship with God and with your loved one?

2   When are your prayers the most honest and open? Why? How is your prayer experience different when you pray more authentically? Does it change the outcome?

3   When do you find it most difficult to trust God? What spiritual practices, prayers or Bible verses help you continue to trust God when you are angry, confused or hurting?

4   Where do you most clearly sense God's presence in your life today? How does slowing down and remaining open to God allow you to notice God's presence and provision?

5   Why do you think we want to have all the answers and be in control? Who or what gives you the courage to place everything in God's hands?

Wednesday 12 April

1   When someone asks you to do something difficult, how do you respond? Has a scripture passage ever made you change your response like it did for today's writer? If so, what was the passage? How did it change your response?

2   Do you ever fear that you don't have enough to offer anything to others? What motivates you to share what you have anyway? What happens when you do?

3   When do you feel most in need of God's provision? When are you most aware of God's provision? Is it ever easy for you to lose sight of all that God provides? Why or why not?

4   What stories from scripture show you the importance of following God's call to care for others? How do you apply the lessons you learn from those stories to your life?

5   In what ways have you been blessed by caring for those around you or by receiving the care of others? How do you remain open to God's call to care for others each day?

Wednesday 19 April

1   When you feel overwhelmed or fearful, what physical locations comfort you and help you find peace? What about that place makes you feel safe?

2   What prayers, objects, locations and practices help you experience the comfort of Christ?

3   What peace and hope do you have knowing that through Christ, we all can access the refuge God provides? How does God's refuge get you through difficult times?

4   Describe a time when you were afraid or overwhelmed and found comfort through Christ. Who or what helped you experience that comfort?

5   Why can it be easy to forget about the comfort and safety we have in Christ when life is going well? How do you remain focused on and grateful for that safety in good times and bad times alike?

Wednesday 26 April

1 Recall a time when someone's words comforted you and strengthened your faith. What did their words mean to you?

2 Have you ever experienced a devastating circumstance that eventually gave you a chance to grow in your faith or to help those around you? Explain the situation.

3 Why do you think we tend to question God when we are grieving or when life is not going as we hoped? How does God respond to our questions?

4 What does it mean to you to know that God is grieving and weeping with us? In what ways does it change the way you view grief and the painful circumstances we all experience? In what ways does it change the way you view God?

5 Why is the care of community so important when we are suffering? How does your community support you in times of grief and sorrow? How do you support those around you?

Become a Friend of BRF
and give regularly to support our ministry

We help people of all ages to grow in faith

We encourage and support individual Christians and churches as they
serve and resource the changing spiritual needs of communities today.

Through **Anna Chaplaincy**
we're enabling churches to provide
spiritual care to older people

Through **Living Faith**
we're nurturing faith and resourcing
lifelong discipleship

Through **Messy Church**
we're helping churches to reach out
to families

Through **Parenting for Faith**
we're supporting parents as they raise
their children in the Christian faith

Our ministry is only possible because of the generous support of
individuals, churches, trusts and gifts in wills.

As we look to the future and make plans, **regular donations make a huge
difference** in ensuring we can both start and finish projects well.

By becoming a Friend of BRF and giving regularly to our ministry you are
partnering with us in the gospel and helping change lives.

How your gift makes a difference

£2 a month — Helps us to give away **Living Faith** resources via food banks and chaplaincy services

£10 a month — Helps us to support parents and churches running the **Parenting for Faith** course

£5 a month — Helps us to support **Messy Church** volunteers and grow the wider network

£20 a month — Helps us to develop the reach of **Anna Chaplaincy** and improve spiritual care for older people

How to become a Friend of BRF

Online – set up a Direct Debit donation at **brf.org.uk/donate** or find out how to set up a Standing Order at **brf.org.uk/friends**

By post – complete and return the tear-off form opposite to 'Freepost BRF' (*no other address or stamp is needed*)

If you have any questions, or if you want to change your regular donation or stop giving in the future, do get in touch.

Contact the fundraising team

Email: **giving@brf.org.uk**
Tel: 01235 462305
Post: Fundraising team, BRF, 15 The Chambers, Vineyard, Abingdon OX14 3FE

Registered with
FUNDRAISING
REGULATOR

Bible Reading Fellowship (BRF) is a charity (233280) and company limited by guarantee (301324), registered in England and Wales

I would like to make a donation to support BRF.
Please use my gift for:

☐ Where the need is greatest ☐ Anna Chaplaincy ☐ Living Faith
☐ Messy Church ☐ Parenting for Faith

Title	First name/initials	Surname

Address

	Postcode

Email

Telephone

Signature		Date

Our ministry is only possible because of the generous support of individuals, churches, trusts and gifts in wills.

Please treat as Gift Aid donations all qualifying gifts of money made

giftaid it

☐ today, ☐ in the past four years, ☐ and in the future.

I am a UK taxpayer and understand that if I pay less Income Tax and/or Capital Gains Tax in the current tax year than the amount of Gift Aid claimed on all my donations, it is my responsibility to pay any difference.

☐ My donation does not qualify for Gift Aid.

Please notify BRF if you want to cancel this Gift Aid declaration, change your name or home address, or no longer pay sufficient tax on your income and/or capital gains.

You can also give online at **brf.org.uk/donate**, which reduces our administration costs, making your donation go further.

Please complete other side of form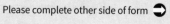

SHARING OUR VISION – MAKING A GIFT

Please accept my gift of:

☐ £2 ☐ £5 ☐ £10 ☐ £20 Other £ [　　　　　]

by (*delete as appropriate*):

☐ Cheque/Charity Voucher payable to 'BRF'

☐ MasterCard/Visa/Debit card/Charity card

Name on card

Card no. ☐☐☐☐ ☐☐☐☐ ☐☐☐☐ ☐☐☐☐ ☐☐☐☐

Expires end [M M] [Y Y] Security code [☐☐☐] Last 3 digits on the reverse of the card

Signature ┊ Date

☐ I would like to leave a gift to BRF in my will.
Please send me further information.

For help or advice regarding making a gift, please contact
our fundraising team +44 (0)1865 462305

Your privacy

We will use your personal data to process this transaction.
From time to time we may send you information about the
work of BRF that we think may be of interest to you. Our
privacy policy is available at **brf.org.uk/privacy**. Please
contact us if you wish to discuss your mailing preferences.

Registered with

FUNDRAISING
REGULATOR

➥ Please complete other side of form

Please return this form to 'Freepost BRF'
No other address information or stamp is needed

BRF

Bible Reading Fellowship is a charity (233280) and company limited by guarantee (301324),
registered in England and Wales

UR0123

Lent is traditionally a time of repentance, fasting and prayer as we prepare to celebrate our salvation at Easter. Through daily readings and reflections from Ash Wednesday to Easter Day, Amy Scott Robinson explores different biblical images of repentance, sin, forgiveness and grace, bringing them together in Holy Week as a lens through which to view Christ's work of reconciliation on the cross.

Images of Grace
A journey from darkness to light at Easter
Amy Scott Robinson
978 1 80039 117 8 £9.99
brfonline.org.uk

Across a year's worth of weekly reflections, Gordon Giles focuses on objects, scenes, activities and places, drawing out spiritual insights to help us reflect on what we have learned as we venture out again after months of restriction, absence and anxiety. From Easter, through the changing seasons to the following Easter, we are led to consider where is Christ amid our restrictions and our releases?

At Home and Out and About
52 biblical contemplations on faith, hope and love for a re-emerging world
Gordon Giles
978 1 80039 115 4 £9.99
brfonline.org.uk

How to encourage Bible reading in your church

BRF has been helping individuals connect with the Bible for 100 years. We want to support churches as they seek to encourage church members into regular Bible reading.

Order a Bible reading resources pack

This pack is designed to give your church the tools to publicise our Bible reading notes. It includes:

- Sample Bible reading notes for your congregation to try.
- Publicity resources, including a poster.
- A church magazine feature about Bible reading notes.

The pack is free, but we welcome a £5 donation to cover the cost of postage. If you require a pack to be sent outside the UK or require a specific number of sample Bible reading notes, please contact us for postage costs. For more information about what the current pack contains, go to **brfonline.org.uk/pages/bible-reading-resources-pack**.

How to order and find out more

- Email **enquiries@brf.org.uk**
- Telephone BRF on +44 (0)1865 319700 Mon–Fri 9.30–17.00
- Write to us at BRF, 15 The Chambers, Vineyard, Abingdon OX14 3FE.

Keep informed about our latest initiatives

We are continuing to develop resources to help churches encourage people into regular Bible reading, wherever they are on their journey. Join our email list at **brfonline.org.uk/signup** to stay informed about the latest initiatives that your church could benefit from.

Subscriptions

The Upper Room is published in January, May and September.

Individual subscriptions
The subscription rate for orders for 4 or fewer copies includes postage and packing:

The Upper Room annual individual subscription   £19.05

Group subscriptions
Orders for 5 copies or more, sent to ONE address, are post free:
The Upper Room annual group subscription   £14.85

Please do not send payment with order for a group subscription.
We will send an invoice with your first order.

Please note that the annual billing period for group subscriptions runs from 1 May to 30 April.

Copies of the notes may also be obtained from Christian bookshops.

Single copies of *The Upper Room* cost £4.95.

Prices valid until 30 April 2024.

Giant print version
The Upper Room is available in giant print for the visually impaired, from:

Torch Trust for the Blind
Torch House
Torch Way
Northampton Road
Market Harborough   Tel: +44 (0)1858 438260
LE16 9HL   **torchtrust.org**

**All our Bible reading notes can be ordered online by visiting
brfonline.org.uk/subscriptions**

☐ I would like to take out a subscription myself (complete your name
and address details once)

☐ I would like to give a gift subscription (please provide both names
and addresses)

Title .... First name/initials .... Surname ....

Address ....

.... Postcode ....

Telephone .... Email ....

Gift subscription name ....

Gift subscription address ....

.... Postcode ....

Gift message (20 words max. or include your own gift card):

....

....

Please send *The Upper Room* beginning with the May 2023 /
September 2023 / January 2024 issue (*delete as appropriate*):

Annual individual subscription ☐ £19.05

Optional donation* to support the work of BRF £ ....

Total enclosed £ .... (cheques should be made payable to 'BRF')

*Please complete and return the Gift Aid declaration on page 159 to make your
 donation even more valuable to us.

Method of payment

Please charge my MasterCard / Visa with £ ....

Card no. ☐☐☐☐ ☐☐☐☐ ☐☐☐☐ ☐☐☐☐

Expires end ☐☐ ☐☐ Security code ☐☐☐ Last 3 digits on the
reverse of the card

**All our Bible reading notes can be ordered online by visiting
brfonline.org.uk/subscriptions**

❏ Please send me .... copies of *The Upper Room* May 2023 /
September 2023 / January 2024 issue (*delete as appropriate*)

Title .... First name/initials .... Surname ....

Address ....

.... Postcode ....

Telephone .... Email ....

Please do not send payment with this order. We will send an invoice with
your first order.

Christian bookshops: All good Christian bookshops stock BRF publications.
For your nearest stockist, please contact BRF.

Telephone: The BRF office is open Mon–Fri 9.30–17.00. To place your order,
telephone +44 (0)1865 319700.

Online: brfonline.org.uk/group-subscriptions

❏ Please send me a Bible reading resources pack to encourage Bible
reading in my church

Please return this form with the appropriate payment to:
BRF, 15 The Chambers, Vineyard, Abingdon OX14 3FE

For terms and cancellation information, please visit **brfonline.org.uk/terms**.

Bible Reading Fellowship is a charity (233280) and company limited by guarantee (301324),
registered in England and Wales

UR0123

Delivery times within the UK are normally 15 working days. Prices are correct at the time of going to press but may change without prior notice.

itle	Price	Qty	Total
mages of Grace (BRF Lent book 2023)	£9.99		
t Home and Out and About	£9.99		

POSTAGE AND PACKING CHARGES			
der value	UK	Europe	Rest of world
nder £7.00	£2.00		
.00–£29.99	£3.00	Available on request	Available on request
0.00 and over	FREE		

Total value of books	
Postage and packing	
Donation*	
Total for this order	

ease complete in BLOCK CAPITALS

* Please complete the Gift Aid declaration below

Title .... First name/initials .... Surname...............................

Address...

.... Postcode ....

Acc. No. .... Telephone ....

Email ....

Gift Aid Declaration

giftaid it

Please treat as Gift Aid donations all qualifying gifts of money made (*tick all that apply*) ❑ today, ❑ in the past four years, ❑ and in the future **or** ❑ My donation does not qualify for Gift Aid.

am a UK taxpayer and understand that if I pay less Income Tax and/or Capital Gains Tax in the current tax year than the amount of Gift Aid claimed on all my donations, it is my responsibility o pay any difference.

Please notify BRF if you want to cancel this declaration, change your name or home address, or no longer pay sufficient tax on your income and/or capital gains.

Method of payment

❑ Cheque (made payable to BRF) ❑ MasterCard / Visa

Card no. ⬜⬜⬜⬜ ⬜⬜⬜⬜ ⬜⬜⬜⬜ ⬜⬜⬜⬜

Expires end ⬜⬜ M M ⬜⬜ Y Y Security code ⬜⬜⬜ Last 3 digits on the reverse of the card

ease return this form to:

RF, 15 The Chambers, Vineyard, Abingdon OX14 3FE | **enquiries@brf.org.uk** r terms and cancellation information, please visit **brfonline.org.uk/terms**.

Enabling all ages to grow in faith

Anna Chaplaincy

Living Faith

Messy Church

Parenting for Faith

BRF is a Christian charity that resources individuals and churches. Our vision is to enable people of all ages to grow in faith and understanding of the Bible and to see more people equipped to exercise their gifts in leadership and ministry.

To find out more about our work, visit

brf.org.uk